UPSIDE OF DOWN

HOW INTENTIONALLY GOING LOWER CAN TAKE YOU HIGHER

By:

Kenneth S. Albin

Accolades and Endorsements for Upside of Down

Humility is a strange thing. As soon as you think and start talking about your humility you stop being humble. Humility is an outward manifestation of the posture of your heart. The greatest example of humility in the Bible is when Jesus humbled Himself (Philippians 2:8) to leave the portals of heaven, come to earth and die for our sins. We are beneficiaries of His humility. Humility is internal—it's an intentional way of living. My friend Pastor Ken Albin in his book The Upside of Down, captures the principles, processes and products of humility. Read this book not just for information but transformation.
—**Dr. Samuel R. Chand, author of Cracking Your Church's Culture Code**

Pastor Ken Albin has written a very powerful and long over due book. "The Upside of Down," stirred my heart to deep conviction and solace in who God is raising up. Humility is the key to the kingdom. It is what opens the door for the supernatural. Ken shows the heart of God as he walks the reader through this lost fruit of the Spirit! I honestly believe that this book is a plumb line for the victorious and the miraculous! When you pick it up get prepared for it to put you on your knees! God will use this book to restore the heart of the shepherd, and the much needed voice of the church! I am deeply honored to say, "Get this book and consume every word of it!"—**Patrick Schatzline, Evangelist, author of Why Is God so mad at Me?**

Humility… it is one of the most powerful character-traits a person can possess. And, although it can be difficult to define, it is certainly obvious whenever it is present. In Upside of Down, not only has Ken brought fresh perspective, practicality and understanding on how to live the strong and rewarding life of humility, but he also models it in his everyday life.—**Lead Pastor Scott Thomas, Free Life Chapel, Lakeland, Florida**

Ken Albin has an interesting perspective into the interpretive tension described in James 4:6, that presents the idea that God resists the proud, yet gives grace to the humble. He uses this text to launch deeply into exploring what he calls the "Upside of Down". Feeding from his pastoral experience, Ken dissects the idea of humility as the key- stone for achieving success in life and effectiveness in biblical living. His insights are appealing to the mind, heart and soul of any leader.—**Dr. Marc Rivera**

As my friend and Author of the book Humble for President, Jeremie Kubicek says; "Humility is an ancient, quiet and unvarnished virtue that has the potential to transform not only our politics, but our everyday lives and leadership. "I couldn't' agree with Jeremie more and so I'm thrilled to see Ken Albin expounding on the little known, super-natural power of humble in his latest book. The Upside of Down is a must read for anyone who truly desires to emulate one of Jesus' most powerful leadership attributes.—Kevin Weaver, author of Re-Orient You'll See An Uprising

The one thing about dear and precious Ken Albin is steadfastness to obey God and stay at His feet! We have watched Ken go through the fire of God's presence to come out purified and made ready. Many would have given up, but we have watched as he has gone lower in the spirit of humble into now a glorious victory. I believe ken has heard from heaven and is flowing through the Spirit of God to write these words to bring healing, health, and life back to the last days' prophetic church! Thank you for obeying His voice & writing this timely book, Upside of Down. Thank you for penning these words that can bring life, change, hope, and healing once again. Thank you for always staying low to His feet, so that only He is seen. You have hit the mark in the Spirit of God once again!—**Harry and Cheryl Salem, national best-selling authors and speakers**

This book is full of wisdom and has applicable nuggets about humility. Don't expect this to be about the average view on humility, but rather, it is an eye opener of the many different facets of being humble. I recommend this book to every Christian that wants to strengthen their walk with the Lord.—**Mikel French, evangelist, author**

In his book, 'The Upside of Down', Pastor Ken Albin paints an incredible picture of what true servant-hood looks like.

In a 'me, me, me society' there are still some chosen people who have learned and experienced the UPside of Down. They have learned as Jesus taught, "Whoever wants to be the greatest among you, let him be the servant of all." In this book you will learn strategies, real-life experiences from someone who has walked this walk and has come out on the other side. Pastor Ken is a truly anointed servant of the Most High God and is a servant to God's people and for His kingdom. Read and learn how to experience the "UPside of Down", —**Pastor Judy Jacobs, worship leader/psalmist/author**

The key to personal power and the abiding presence of God is found in humility. However, the truth of that statement is seldom addressed in a powerful and life giving revelation. Ken Albin has given us a blueprint for powerful living within the pages of this book, THE UPSIDE OF DOWN. he new believer will find courage in their journey. The seasoned believer will be renewed in their commitment to Christlikeness. This impacting and life- changing book can be studied individually or in a group setting. The power of this truth is desperately needed in the body of Christ today. Thoughtful and well written, this book reminds us that doing things God's way, produces God's results. —**Dr. Shirley Arnold, Author, Apostle Revival People Network**

DEDICATION

I WOULD LIKE to dedicate this book to my life partner and love of my life for now over thirty-one years, my beloved girl- friend Lisa. When we met and fell in love as teenagers in your grandfather's church youth group, I could never have imagined what life would be like with someone so special. Your faith in God is contagious, a faith that has kept me connected to our God in the center of our life together. I love your boldness and your exciting and positive personality in the face of so much craziness. I am completely blown away that you would give me your heart, so precious it is and so tender. I only want the best for you and of course our perfect daughter, Brittney. When this book and message was poured through me, it was you who not only believe in this message but your life is the epitome of the message in this book. I believe with all my heart that God will restore double to you all that was lost or stolen and great mega grace will be attracted to your humble spirit. There is no one in this world I love or admire more. If I say that you are the "wind beneath my wings," it would be a gross understatement because you aren't just my wind, you are my wings! With all my love and appreciativeness, I dedicate this book to you.

Contents

Foreword
Upside of Down: How Intentionally Going Lower
Can Take Your Higher!
The Humble Principle
Can You Hear Me Now?
What's Killing Today's Church?
The Humble Upside of Down Life
A Long and Slow Death!
A Humble Lower Always Leads to Higher
Jesus Teaching on Humble
Reigning As Child Kings
The Inheritance Only Grace Can Give
Humble Love
No Vacancy!
The Humble Church
My Upside of Down Journey
Notes
About the Author

FOREWORD BY DR. MARK CHIRONNA

THE COUNTERCULTURAL REVOLUTION of the 1960s has had a profound effect on the twenty-first century in ways many people are not conscious of. The radical revolution that started as an antiestablishment movement among a rising generation of teens and twenty-somethings led to what became known back then as the generation gap. Lots of powerful things emerged in the culture that have changed us for the better. Civil Rights, issues of ecology and the environment, social justice and fairness issues, renewed vigor in rights for women, and many other necessary shifts began to take place. We still have a long way to go; however, there were things that history reveals would never have happened apart from the young radical revolutionaries that spawned a whole new conscious- ness across the nation and in the Western world. At the same time, consumerism began to increase and expand, and it seems as if everyone felt they wanted their share in the piece of the pie known as the American Dream. As wonderful as that may be, there was an unexpected fruit born of the blossoming consumer-driven culture. It was what Tom Wolfe described regarding many of the baby boomers born between 1946 and 1964; he named them the me generation because of the tendency toward a high degree of self-centeredness and "what's in it for me" belief systems and values. It has been said that what one-generation allows in moderation the next generation excuses in excess.

Today there is a real tendency for the current age to be filled with blatant yet unrecognized narcissism. To say that is it only in the secular culture is to live with blinders on or at the least with only one eye opened. In fact, you could say, the denial of the narcissistic bent in the current culture is in fact the blind spot of the age we live in. With extreme "what's in it for me" beliefs, the ego sits enthroned and the universe is then believed to revolve around the ego. With that ego- driven, needs-driven approach to life, entitlement abounds in almost every area of human experience, and people lose their ability to stay grounded. To be grounded is to be close to the earth. The word for who we are is "human beings." The etymology of the word "human" comes from the word "humus," which is tied to the earth. In fact, it is tied to being close to the dirt from which we were all derived. The "what's in it for me" mentality has invaded the church in the twenty-first century, and we have lost our ability to be rooted and grounded in Christ. The Hebrew word for being made from the "humus" or "the earth" is the name of the father of the human race, "Adam" or "adamah" in Hebrew, which means, "ground." The word "humility" and the word "humble" come from the same root words as all of these words. To be humble is to be in a posture in life that keeps you grounded because you stay low to the dirt from which you came. There is no ego-inflation or egocentricity when humility is valued. It is the one thing that God looks for in us, that if we fail to do, namely to humble ourselves, his hand cannot exalt us. In fact, the hand that exalts the humble by lifting them up is the hand that opposes the proud by pressing them down closer to the ground so that they will be reminded of where they came from. Pastor Ken Albin in Upside of Down has lifted his voice in prophetic concern and passion for a generation to begin to recapture the grace and the power of humility. Take time to feed on his insights and his instructions, and let the Spirit use Ken Albin's insights to keep you grounded, and humble, so that in due season, God can exalt you.

—Bishop Mark J. Chironna, MA, PhD
Mark Chironna Ministries Church on the Living Edge

INTRODUCTION

THIS BOOK IS about an ancient truth that, for the most part, man has been blinded to. The secret is found in both the Old and New Testaments of the Bible and has to do with the greatest blessings in life being either attracted to or repelled from us. The blessings of God are available to the people who know how to attract the power of grace. Unfortunately, because God is no respecter of persons, he will resist or be repelled from those who don't. We know about natural laws such as gravity, or the law of lift, but we don't know much about the laws of the Spirit. These also work whether you believe them or not, understand them or not, just like the natural earthy laws. I like to call these laws of the spirit technology of the soul. This technology is something we need to embrace because it will help us do and live this life so much better. Since we have only one life, we ought to always be in a state of learning and growing. As a lifelong student continue to feed your spirit and your soul. After formal education, you should be learning and growing from the people you meet, the books you read, and the teachers you receive into your life. The hidden truth and the premise of this book is that "God will resist the people who are proud, but will give grace to those who are humble" (James 4:6). If you don't want God to fight against you and grace be repelled from your life then make sure there isn't a drop or scent of pride in your life, because it will keep God and grace far away. For those who will humble themselves, the grace that brings every blessing will be attracted to you and find you wherever you are. Let me tell you a true story that will enhance and give a picture of how desperately we need this soul technology in our lives.

One night I had the privilege of being in a men's mentoring small group at my church where the young and the not-so-young gather to learn from God's Word and from each other how to dispel the lies that men believe. Each man shared their thoughts on their fathers or lack of them. One young man in particular shared how his father had never been involved in his life in any way. His parents don't live together and haven't for quite sometime. The young man shared his experience of how at twelve for the first time he went to visit his father. When he arrived, he asked his dad, "Why haven't you been there for me all these years?" Immediately his father punched him in the chest and told him, "Stop being so sensitive!" When the boy continued to press him, the father then punched the young boy in the face and said, "Stop asking me about the past. You see me now, you should be happy!" The young boy and his father actually got into a fistfight that resulted in the house a wreck and the little, confused boy back on a plane home.

As the young man told the story, he was heartbroken and dealing years later with great desperation as he said, "How can anyone really love me when my own dad rejected me?" As I write this, my heart is broken for the young man who has a father that would not humble himself to his son who needed him so critically. Now, I know this story might not be unique, but it demonstrates that, today without the hidden power of humble, there will continue to be stories like this one. How many marriages end up in divorce because not one of the partners will humble themselves for the sake of the marriage and future? They would rather be full of pride and reap the rewards of rejection, disillusionment, and disappointment. I believe most relationships and families can be healed when at least one will lower and humble themselves to see the upside of down. You see, when you humble yourself it doesn't mean you're weak.

When you humble yourself it doesn't mean you're giving in to bad behaviors or saying the way you're being treated is just or fair.

 When you humble yourself it doesn't mean you're giving in to bad behaviors or saying the way you're being treated is just or fair. This is the struggle most people have with the very idea of humble. They believe if they humble themselves, then they are giving up their power, when actually they are releasing a greater force than they can imagine.

When I talk about the upside of down, I am talking about going higher through a soul technology I call the principle of humble. I want you to see and experience real power available for every nook and cranny of your life. Are you struggling with financial or career issues? What about how to deal with a co-worker, employee, or someone over you in your business? What if you could tap into a secret, hidden power that would help you navigate through the slippery slopes and potentially potent paths that are common to all of us mere humans? I think about all the movies that are popular depicting a super- hero that has superpowers whenever they need it. Sometimes I wish I could use my superpowers to change the world. How about you? If I could, I would fix every marriage. I would do it in the blink of an eye. World hunger would be a distant memory. Lack of any and every kind, gone! If I had those superpowers, what a different world it would be. I know you would probably do the same thing. We all would make the world a better place if we could. But what if there was a power available to us as mere humans, and we just didn't know about it or weren't taught how to use it? Is it possible that there are hidden treasures waiting to be discovered or, like I say, uncovered for all of our benefit and enjoyment? Think how the ability to use the principles and substances found beneath the earth are now used in technology such as the smart phone and other devices that help us connect to one another and make our lives better. Haven't these substances been in the earth before you and I were born? Are they new substances and new principles or have they just been uncovered, discovered, and presented in new ways?

In the book of Daniel it says, "Knowledge shall increase" (Daniel 12:4.) Knowledge is the Hebrew word rabah, which has the meaning of multiplication and greatly increasing. We've seen the exponential knowledge of man increase and multiply so fast it's almost impossible to keep up with what is happening so rapidly. Right now, there is also and expansion of knowledge taking place in medicine, agriculture, and science. But wait! Could there also be knowledge expanding when it comes to how mere humans can tap into a hidden power they haven't even known existed? I believe they can, and will, and that's why I am

4

writing this book Upside of Down. I believe hidden within the pages of the Bible is a principle that has barely been tapped until now. Now, hidden in this truth about humble is the key to unlock the doors to destiny, healing for the hurting and miracles for those who need them the most. This hidden power of "humble" will be given to those who are willing to peek into a box of treasure without just becoming enamored by its beauty and power, and instead, receiving the treasure's true worth when it's used to benefit more than just yourself. I believe what you're about to read and see will not only change your life radically but will transform the world as you take what you learn and impart it to others. I warn you not to be selfish but to share this message with everyone you can. This is a technology for the soul that can benefit all who live their lives with its advantage.

What if everything you wanted in life could really be yours if you only knew how to receive it?

Now, would it interest you to know that unlimited power is available to the humble? I hope I now have your attention. What if everything you wanted in life could really be yours if you only knew how to receive it? Did you notice I didn't say take it? I said it was available to those who receive. Today many people have been taught to take or they won't have. They have been told to "Go for it! Make it happen! Get all you can then can all you get!" I've been a believer in Christ for over thirty years, and even good church people have bought the lie of self-exaltation and self-gratification, making sure self is always satisfied by taking rather than receiving. I have witnessed many leaders lift his or her own selves up rather than let God do it in his time. I promise you

I am not bashing the church. I love the church and have given my life for the sheep as a pastor. Do you realize that a Christian never has to lift himself up to get to the top? In fact, I believe the moment you start making yourself known, boasting, bragging, and of course, bashing everyone else around, you actually are on your way down. I don't believe it's wrong to want to go higher, be recognized, valued, or appreciated. It's the "how" that I will talk about in this book and why it's so important that you and I learn the majestic beauty and power of living humbly in a world that that is full of pride. I believe with all my heart that being humble is a key and a foundation to receive everything you have ever wanted in life and more! The upside of down comes to those who learn how to live in this soul technology of humble. The upside of down is activated when you intentionally make yourself lower so God can take you higher.

Jesus said in John 10:10 that he "came to give us a rich and satisfying and overflowing life." If Jesus came to give this abundant, overflowing life here on the earth, is it wrong to desire it? Actually, so many scriptures in the Bible promise us a full life. Psalms 37 promises us that we will live full, healthy lives, and if we delight ourselves in the Lord, even our hearts desires will be given to us.

The life that God came to give us is available to every person who understands one of the hidden truths of the Bible. This truth is a hidden key that will unlock the wonderful, powerful plan God has for you and those connected to you. Knowing and applying this key will not only change you but those around you. It's my heart and prayer that as you read this book, your life will be radically altered for the better. It's my prayer that as you read this book, your eyes will be opened to a way of life that will attract favor and blessing to you like never before. Now I know some of you who are reading this are already so blessed, but if there's more for you, I'm sure you desire the more I'm talking about. The scriptures teach that everything God does increases. One of my favorite verses in the Bible is, "May the Lord give you increase more and more, you and your children." (Psalms 115:14, NKJV)

I also love these scriptures:

But we all, with unveiled face, beholding as in a mirror the glory of the Lord, are being transformed into the same image from glory to glory, just as by the Spirit of the Lord. 2 Corinthians 3:18 (NKJV) both of these scriptures show that whatever God does is always moving forward and increasing. God is never stagnant or passive. God is a proactive God, "Calling those things that aren't as though they have already existed." Romans 4:17 (NKJV)

The upside of down is that when you make yourself lower and humble, God will take you higher than you ever could have imagined!

What would you say if I told you I thought most of what we've heard about humble is wrong? We've gotten "humble" so messed up, I'm tempted not to put my picture on the front of the book because if I do, many will say, "How can he write a book about humble and then not be humble putting his picture on the cover?" You know I'm right! You thought that, didn't you? You might even be reading this book just to figure out how a humble person could put his picture on the cover of a book that is about

7

going lower and being humble. I believe most people don't really know what humble is, and we tend to make erroneous assumptions based on what we've heard about being humble. What you and I have probably heard about humility and humble people is most likely wrong. I know growing up I always thought of humble as weakness. I thought humble people would always live a life of poverty and doing without. In my mind, they were humble if they were poor and gave every- thing they had to others and took no thought of themselves. Wrong! Wrong! Wrong! Did you get that? I couldn't have been more wrong. Humility doesn't mean you're weak or don't think about yourself. It's not about poverty, giving up prestige or one's possessions. You see the upside of down is that when you make yourself lower and humble, God will take you higher than you ever could have imagined.

In this book, you'll discover what going lower and humble truly means. It's spoken of in the Bible many times, and I can assure you it's anything but weak and poor. I want you to have this secret power of humble in your life. I want you to learn what it is and how this, what I call soul technology, will not only benefit you, but all you connect with. I'm so excited to share what I've received from the Lord about this hidden and powerful truth. I'm not going to oversell you, so I invite you now to read for yourself. I pray as you turn the pages of this book that God would give you the Spirit of revelation and illuminate his Word to you. I pray the Holy Spirit will teach you what you need to know, apply and how to live and experience the upside of down and experience a technology for your soul that will radically change you, your relationships, your family, your finances and your posterity. Get ready, your future will be forever altered by learning how to intentionally go lower so you can go higher than you ever dreamed, imagined or thought possible. I believe you are ready? So let's begin.

CHAPTER ONE:

The Humble Principle

I CAN REMEMBER growing up as a good Jewish boy my mom would always tell everyone she could that her son, Kenny, was perfect. She would be so bold, and frankly, I was always so embarrassed when she said, "My son, Kenny, is perfect." Now if you don't know anything about a Jewish mother, you won't understand how important it is for them to affirm their sons. They do this usually by going way overboard bragging and boasting about how good-looking and smart their sons are, especially if they are their first born. If you're a Jewish boy reading this right now, you know exactly what I'm talking about. If you don't, you're thinking, "Wow, that Jewish boy must have gotten a real big head and grew up very arrogant. His mother sure did a number on him." Truthfully, I joke and say the same thing all the time, "My mom sure did a number on me."

Well, actually in my case it's the opposite that occurred. I didn't grow up thinking I was better, smarter, and more confident in any way, even though my mom certainly told me that

I, Kenny Albin, was "perfect." (Now, Mom, if you're reading this right now, please shut your eyes.) Okay, now let's move on. The fact is just because you were told how great you are doesn't mean you will grow up proud and arrogant. Jesus was greatly affirmed by his Father when he was humbly submit- ting himself to the authority of John by being baptized by him. Let's read together the story:

One day Jesus came from Nazareth in Galilee, and John baptized him in the Jordan River. As Jesus came up out of the water, he saw the heavens splitting apart and the Holy Spirit descending on him like a dove. And a voice from heaven said, "You are my dearly loved Son, and you bring me great joy."
Mark 1:9–11 (NLT)

Jesus had a good Jewish daddy who boasted about his first-born Son too. The heavenly Father didn't hesitate to say good things about his Son. He was bragging and boasting about how Jesus was so loved and how Jesus brought the Father such great joy. Now think about it, there's really nothing wrong with what my mother did to me especially in light of how the Father affirmed his beloved child Jesus. In fact, I believe all children, and yes, all of God's children need to be bragged on and affirmed. They need to feel the love of their parents. They need to know that they are special and a one of a kind masterpiece. They need to be encouraged to soar like eagles and never be demeaned, demoted or denied their heritage as a beloved son or daughter.

Unfortunately, most of us haven't been raised spiritually or physically with this kind of father or mother. Most people, even in the church, live like they're orphans and are trying to earn the respect and love that's already been given. It's sort of the same type of lie in Genesis 3:4 with the first man and woman, Adam and Eve, whom Satan tells, "The reason God doesn't want you to eat the tree of knowledge and good and evil is because you will be like God if you eat it." The deception was that Adam and Eve were already created and made in God's image, and Satan was so envious of that he convinced them they needed something more than they already had or were. This is the same tactic being used today to convince God's sons and daughters that they need to do more, strive for more in their own strength and abilities, thus negating the free gift and good news of the gospel. It is finished, paid in full, and everything you have is a free gift of God's grace. Well, more on that subject later, but for now, I want you to get this powerful principle of humble. You see, the more you know your love and worth as a son or daughter, the more you can rest in what God has already put in you. So you see, even though my mother told me I was perfect, I wasn't arrogant or self-conceited growing up hearing all that my mom would say about me. In the same way, the more we hear what our heavenly Father has done for us and given us through Christ, it won't make us arrogant or self-conceited. Rather, it will actually do the opposite and humble us.

You see, the reason it has the opposite effect is, when the One who created you tells you about all the good you have inside, it can only point to one thing; what you have inside of you has simply been received or given. You didn't work for it, earn it, or even deserve it. You didn't get it because of who you are but whose you are. It's a gift given by inheritance. Later in the book, we'll go into detail about the inheritance only grace can give, but for now understand that everything you have as a child of God has been given because of your relation- ship with God through Jesus. Jesus as the firstborn Son has secured rights and privileges for all of us, which he freely gives us. These are gifts of love that we freely receive according to the scriptures:

What then shall we say to these things? If God is for us, who can be against us? He who did not spare His own Son, but delivered Him up for us all, how shall He not with Him also freely give us all things? Romans 8:31–32 (NKJV)

The foundation of the humble principle is rooted in the strength and unfailing love of the Father for you!

Do you see the last part "He not with Him also freely give us all things"? It's a rhetorical and almost ridiculous question. If the Father has given his most precious and most prized, perfect Son, then will he hold back anything else from us, from the ones he calls his beloved children? The Word of God is a love letter from the Father to you. His love letter is passionately pursuing and always giving grace to those who will receive his abundance. The heart of your heavenly Father is always abounding toward his beloved children. Now I know many of God's people have a hard time with this love and receiving the best that he has. That is one of the reasons I'm writing this book. In America, we are seeing he fruit of the lack of loving parents, especially the lack of true fathers from where identity is supposed to come. Because many have grown up either fatherless or with warped and unbiblical relationships with those who were called to nurture and love them, we see many people doubting the love God has for them. This also many times translates into a child always searching for or trying to earn affirmation in a myriad of relationship settings and situations, mostly which turn out to be either unhealthy or unscriptural in their foundations and application for real free living.

The foundation of the humble principle is rooted in the strength and unfailing love of the Father for you. It's in and through this love that the principle of humble will thrive and work in a powerful way for those of you who will learn its hidden power. For those who resist this, you'll find yourself spending your whole life trying to get something that God wants you to have more than you can even imagine. I'm talking about the inner desire we all have for true greatness, feeling complete and accomplishing the purposes for which we are born. This humble principle is a technology for the soul that I want you to embrace. The humble principle begins with a simple trust in your Creator, the God who has made a way for us through Christ who said:

Do not cling to Me, for I have not yet ascended to My Father; but go to My brethren and say to them, "I am ascending to My Father and your Father, and to My God and your God."

John 20:17 (NKJV)

Through Jesus, the heavenly Father will be your Father if you'll be humble and freely receive all he has already provided. I know what you're thinking right now, "Will you please tell me what the humble principle is?"

The humble principle is this:

Power is never in my own ability but in God's strength that comes by lowering and humbling myself, intentionally making room for grace.

Now I want you to think about that statement as we look at a few scriptures. The first is so key and is found in the book of James (and also in 1 Peter 5):

God resists the proud, but gives grace to the humble.

James 4:6B (NKJV)

Now at first glance we don't really get it, and I'm going to admit that I didn't get this until very recently, and hence, that's why I feel I have to write this book. Now, I love God's grace, but I must admit I thought I was starting to get it until I saw this profound and hidden truth. Do you know that according to the scriptures there's one person that grace can't help? I'm not talking about Satan right now. We know he won't ever be saved. I'm talking about the people who have this one attribute that God's grace absolutely cannot get through. I hope I have your attention because the humble principle comes with a hidden power that only can come to those who are humble. In fact, the more humble you are, the more you get this power. Unfortunately, the reciprocal of this humility is what only grace cannot break through. I promise you I'm not teaching heresy here, just plain Bible. Sometimes the most powerful truths of God's

15

Word are occasionally missed, glossed over, or not fully comprehended. This I believe is true in what both the Old and New Testaments teach about pride and grace. "God resists the proud, but gives grace to the humble" (1 Peter 5:5, James 4:6, Proverbs 3:34).

Another way of looking at this scripture is like this: "Pride repels grace, humble attracts grace." Do you get what the Word teaches? The more pride there is, the less grace there is, the more humility there is, the more grace there is! I have to admit after being saved over thirty years and going to Bible college, seminary, and studying God's Word, I never realized that the only thing grace couldn't get through was pride. As I write this, I'm thinking about the comic book and movie of Superman where there was only one thing that his power couldn't break through. You know what it was, right? For those of you who aren't sure, it was kryptonite. It was a type of rock that Superman not only couldn't penetrate, but a rock that could destroy his seemingly unstoppable supernatural powers. Do you know there's just one thing and only one kind of person that God's grace can't help? It's the person who is full of pride. Pride is kryptonite to God's grace. It's absolutely the only thing according to the scriptures that God's grace won't be able to help. When a person has pride, the scriptures and even the world say they are "full of pride." Think about that statement. For if you're "full of pride," you have no room in your life for anything else. Pride says you don't need anything or anyone. Everything you have is about you, what you have either taken or earned. According to the Word, the proud have their day and should enjoy it now because it won't last, for it's a life built on sand, and sooner or later, it will be gone. Those who build their lives on pride have built their houses with a very weak foundation that will eventually sink. These words I speak to you aren't incidental additions to your life, homeowner improvements to your standard of living. They are foundational words, words to build a life on. If you work these words into your life, you're like a smart carpenter who built his house on solid rock. Rain poured down, the river flooded, a tornado hit—but nothing moved that house. It was fixed to the rock. "But if you just use my words in Bible studies and don't work them into your life, you're like a stupid carpenter who built his house on the sandy beach. When a storm rolled in and the waves came up, it collapsed like a house of cards" (Matthew 7:24–27, MESSAGE).

Jesus is giving advice and a choice to those who would hear. For many would rather build their own house their way. Already full, they have no room for the humble principle, no room for what only grace can bring. Instead, they repel God's grace, building their lives on the sand. This reminds me of watching the news recently as a giant sinkhole has swallowed up many houses that were built unknowingly over it. I'm sure none of those homeowners could ever imagine their house sinking into that sinkhole when they first moved in or built their home. I know ignorance is bliss but not when you see your home sinking into oblivion. Perhaps we can learn the lesson Jesus is trying to teach us. We all need to pay attention to our foundation. Are we making room for grace or are we already full?

If God doesn't build the house, the builders only build shacks.

Psalm 127:1 (MESSAGE)

"Pride repels grace, humble attracts grace."

Wouldn't you rather have more grace in your life than less? I want to give you some keys to the humble principle, but I want you to first be aware of some of the tactics of the enemy of our soul. He has used these tactics many times and is currently using them on many believers, families and churches.

After all, we don't want to unwittingly give Satan an opening for yet more mischief—we're not oblivious to his sly ways!
2 Corinthians 2:11 (MESSAGE)

According to the scriptures, we are not to be ignorant to what the enemy is doing. This book is being written to combat many of the lies and deceptions being used by Satan to seduce God's people in some of the same ways Israel was seduced by Moab. If you read the story about Balak, the king of Moab, you'll see how he tried to use pseudoprophet by the name of Balaam to curse God's people. Balak offered great sums of money and power to Balaam to curse God's people, but Balaam was forbidden by God to go and even entertain king Balak's offer. After a brief incident with a talking donkey, Balaam goes in disobedience and is asked to curse God's covenant people Israel. Each time Balaam begins his pronouncement, the hand of God comes on him and he blesses Israel, the exact opposite of what Balak desired him to do. Balak was so mad and frustrated with Balaam, but three times Balaam does the opposite and blesses Israel.

Those nations didn't treat you with hospitality on your travels out of Egypt, and on top of that they also hired Balaam son of Beor from Pethor in Mesopotamia to curse you. God, your God, refused to listen to Balaam but turned the curse into a blessing—how God, your God, loves you! Deuteronomy 23:4–6 (The Message)

Every time a curse was supposed to be given, a blessing came out instead. Why? Because of a love that came from God that had nothing to do with behavior, obedience, or a list of do's and don'ts. Now according to the scriptures the children of Israel were recipients of a divine love. The choosing of Israel and their father Abraham was a gift of love and grace, and even in their constant disobedience, that love never failed.

The Lord did not set his heart on you and choose you because you were more numerous than other nations, for you were the smallest of all nations! Rather, it was simply that the Lord loves you, and he was keeping the oath he had sworn to your ancestors. That is why the Lord res- cued you with such a strong hand from your slavery and from the oppressive hand of Pharaoh, king of Egypt. Understand, therefore, that the Lord your God is indeed God. He is the faithful God who keeps his covenant for a thousand generations and lavishes his unfailing love on those who love him and obey his commands.
Deuteronomy 7:7–9 (NLT)

I love to read about God's love for Israel. So many in the church don't get God's love for them. They think they must do something, accomplish something, or earn the Father's love. The simple truth is found in one of the most popular and well-read scriptures.

For God so greatly loved and dearly prized the world that He [even] gave up His only begotten (unique) Son, so that whoever believes in (trusts in, clings to, relies on) Him shall not perish (come to destruction, be lost) but have eternal (everlasting) life.
John 3:16 (AMPLIFIED)

"Tell my people that I love them!"

Sadly, this popular scripture is known only in words as a quote, but not a reality in the Christian life for many of God's people. I can remember as a newborn baby in Christ, saved at fifteen years old, I started going to the church of my wife's grandfather. Everyone called him Papa Woody, a man who had a tremendous testimony of having to quit the ministry in his fifties because of severe heart problems and had a his- tory of always being sick and broke, even though he and his wife loved God tremendously. In the 1980s, Papa Woody had a mighty encounter with God's Word and presence, which left him not only healed, but with a revelation that he didn't have in all the years of ministry before. For the first time Papa Woody realized God's love for him. After this encounter, the Lord led Papa Woody and his wife back into the ministry. Can you guess what his message was? The Lord told him, "Tell my people that I love them!" Papa Woody replied, "Lord, they know you love them. They have John 3:16." The Lord would not relent. He said, "My people don't know that I love them, for if they did, they wouldn't be living like children without a

Father." During every service before he gave his sermon, Papa Woody would have the people put their hand on their hearts and repeat three times, "God loves me!" Truthfully, in all the years I sat and heard that man I was never in a service that someone didn't give his or her life to Jesus. He passed away many years ago, but his legacy of love lives on in my heart. If we only knew how much our Papa God loves us we would live so different. This scripture in Ephesians is so powerful when it comes to having a revelation of the Father's love for us. Take a look:

Then Christ will make his home in your hearts as you trust in him. Your roots will grow down into God's love and keep you strong. And may you have the power to understand, as all God's people should, how wide, how long, how high, and how deep his love is. May you experience the love of Christ, though it is too great to understand fully. Then you will be made complete with all the fullness of life and power that comes from God.
Ephesians 3:17–19 (NLT)

Now, for years, Papa Woody had loved God, yet he was, as he would say, "Sick, broke, busted, and disgusted!" It wasn't that he didn't love God with all his heart, for he did. It wasn't a sin problem that kept him sick and hurting. It was a problem between his ears. Papa Woody didn't know how much Papa God loved him. Now, over thirty years later, not much has changed. The problem between our ears is what we believe in our mind to be true about God. Proverbs 23:7 says, "As a man thinks so is he." If we are what we think and believe, then we need to get some foundational beliefs lined and congruent with the teachings of the Bible. Until we do that, we won't be able to comprehend or walk in the humble principle because we'll never live from a place of rest and receiving but rather a place of striving and achieving. Living humbly is resting and receiving and intentionally making room for grace. This is also the truth behind Upside of Down, because you can't be humble without going higher and be exalted by God. You can only live in this humble when you know how much you are loved. Think about it, Daniel is known as a man who is greatly beloved (Daniel 10:11), and look at how amazing his life was. He's the only one of the remnant that doesn't even go through the fiery furnace trial. Have you ever wondered why these Hebrew children were arrested, bound, and eventually cast into a hot oven to die, and yet Daniel, who is guilty of the same crime of not bowing, isn't even questioned? Could it be possible that Daniel, being the head of all the wise men and now stationed in the king's court, could overt such a fate as Shadrach, Meshach, and Abednego? Perhaps the fourth man in the fire was actually a substitute for Daniel, who should've been in the fire as well, except he understood how much God loved him. It's just a thought, but I believe the more we under- stand how much God loves us, the more we will understand the power of the cross and how Jesus has become our substitute and continually takes our deserved punishment while graciously exchanging what we merited for what he justifies because of his great love.

This is also the truth behind Upside of Down, because you can't be humble without going higher and be exalted by God.

This is what real love is: It is not our love for God; it is God's love for us. He sent his Son to die in our place to take away our sins.
1 John 4:10 (NCV)

Jesus, out of unfailing and underserved love for us, took our place on the cross and suffered like no one has ever suffered to the end, that we might be free from the condemnation and judgment because of our sins. Read this please:

God sent him to die in our place to take away our sins. We receive forgiveness through faith in the blood of Jesus' death. This showed that God always does what is right and fair, as in the past when he was patient and did not punish people for their sins. And God gave Jesus to show today that he does what is right. God did this so he could judge rightly and so he could make right any person who has faith in Jesus.
Romans 3:25–26 (NCV)

The King James Version of this scripture says "He might be just and the justifier of the one who has faith in Jesus." Do you realize that God's love for us is so great that when it comes to salvation and blessing the only thing we must do is learn how to believe and receive what Jesus has already done for us. Is it possible that we too could be like Daniel and not even have to go through the fiery furnaces of life when we understand that Jesus has already taken our place and he loves us radically more than we could ever comprehend? Please don't tune me out here. I believe the hardest thing for a person to really get is unconditional love. This is the agape love that comes only from God, and the Bible says in 1 John 4:8 that "God is love," and this is the foundation not only for the Christian life, but for the power that's received in the humble principle. Let me take this just a little deeper by giving some insight into why most people still are trying to strive and achieve rather than rest and receive.

If most Christians really believed that God loved them, they would live from a place of generosity and abundance rather than scarcity and lack. If they believed in that love, they would give that love out freely to others instead of walking in condemnation for the ones who need Christ's love the most. Have you ever thought or wondered why there seems to be so many haters in the church? I'm convinced that many of these people do love God, but they don't know God's love. According to 1 John if they truly experienced the love of God, they wouldn't be haters. I don't want to spend an absorbent amount of time on haters. I want to see them all become real lovers. Would you think these "haters" are operating in the humble principle and are receiving grace? I think not. I believe they're not only hurting the body of Christ but also themselves. I have a definition of love I believe will help right now. "Love is passionately pursing and giving what is good, gracious, noble, and true." It's impossible to be a hater and operate in God's extravagant love. Can you imagine what would happen if we could see all the haters, who are full already and have no room for grace and love, begin to live humbly? Living in humility attracts God and his grace while pride and hate will repel the very thing we all need and the world is desperately searching for. Because many good church people and those who call themselves Christians haven't moved and flowed in humble, the world has seen the hypocrisy and lack of congruence between a gospel of love we say we preach and the reality of hatred constantly outwardly manifesting the lack of love and humility in the church.

The world today is very savvy and with lightning speed almost nothing we say or do is hidden from being scrutinized by the public.

Since we know, "For the earnest expectation of the creature waiteth for the manifestation of the sons of God" (Romans 8:19, KJV).

What this scripture is alluding to is the fact that right now the world is longing to see true sons and daughters of God who know who they are. I believe these are the humble; the ones who don't strive to achieve, but live in rest and receive all that God has for them. These are those who will live and walk in abundant grace and the free gift of Christ's righteousness (Romans 5:17 NKJV). I want you to be that person who operates and lives in the humble principle. I want to be that person! I want to see a new kind of Christian, a believer who is more like Jesus than ever before. A person who not just says that they love God but knows how to receive God's love for them and be so filled with that love that they ooze the love of God out wherever they are or go. What would happen if we could see a new humble church, resting and receiving, not lifting themselves or pushing a doc- trine, but genuine humbleness before God and man, never lifting themselves or forcing their agenda or plan? I want you to know you are God's beloved the same

25

way Daniel and Jesus knew it. I love the scripture in Revelation where it says:

Unto him that loved us, and washed us from our sins in his own blood.
Revelation 1:5 (KJV)

Living in humility attracts God and his grace while pride and hate will repel the very thing we all need!

I never get tired of hearing about how my Heavenly Father loves me. In fact, as the good Jewish boy my mom trained me to be, I never get tired of hearing how Kenny is perfect. LOL! Now again, I know I'm not perfect except in Christ, but it still warms my soul to know and receive how my mother feels about her son, Kenny. Do you know that right now the Heavenly Father is speaking only good about you? You are the apple of his eye. He knows every hair of your head. He fashioned and formed you and calls you "fearfully and wonderfully made" (Psalm 139:14).

Your Heavenly Father isn't holding back his awesome love. In fact, he's singing over you with love songs constantly with "songs of deliverance" (Psalm 32:7). Can you hear the sound of your beloved? He longs to be near you, for he is ever with you and will forever fight for your good. I want you to put your hand on your heart with me and say just like Papa Woody taught us. Say with me now, "God loves me." Now say it again but make it personal like, "God loves Kenny!" I mean, "God loves_____!" You fill in the blank with your name. Repeat it three times, and remember what the Lord told Papa Woody, "My people don't know I love them." The humble principle starts by making room for God by being humble because "God resists the proud but gives grace to the humble" (1 Peter 5:5, nkjv). By the way, the word in the Greek for "**resists**" is antitassō. This word means that God opposes or ranges in battle against. That is a very strong word. So if you don't want to find yourself fighting God, then maybe it's time we all learn the humble principle.

The humble principle is this:

Power is never in my own ability, but in God's strength that comes by lowering and humbling myself, intentionally making room for grace.

Let's pray! *Heavenly Father, I thank you for your extravagant love for me that you demonstrated when Jesus died on the cross as a substitute for all my sins. Because of Jesus, I now can receive the gift of righteousness that comes only from resting and receiving in his love for me. I will not strive to achieve and buy into the deception of looking to obtain what has already been generously given to me. Jesus, I choose today, not to just love you, but to be a recipient of your extravagant love for me. By that love, I'm filled with the fullness of God. I'm not a hater! I will not be prejudice! I will passionately pursue and give what is good, gracious, noble, and true to all who come in and out of my path and life. Today I no longer strive to achieve but rest in the love of my Father for me. I choose today to be humble and intentionally make room for grace and more grace. The power I live and walk in is not my own. I find my strength in Christ alone, and when I am weak in myself, then I am strong in the Lord and the power of his might. Today I confess grace is attracted to me because I choose to live humbly resting in the Father's love. God loves_____ ! Amen.*

CHAPTER TWO:

Can You Hear Me Now?

BEFORE WE GET too far into this book, I feel like I need to give you some kind of understanding of what humble is and what it isn't.
Webster's definition on humble:

1.   Not proud or haughty: not arrogant or assertive
2.   Reflecting, expressing, or offered in a spirit of deference or submission <a humble apology>
3.   ranking low in a hierarchy or scale: insignificant, unpretentious

I like what the dictionary says, humble isn't which I believe is accurate. Humble is the antithesis of pride and arrogance, and it doesn't display characteristics of self-assertiveness or self-achievement. But let me explain where the adjective is missing a key truth about humble that we might neglect by just looking at the dictionary definition. In addition, I would like us to glance at what the Bible says about the word humble. The very first time the word humble is mentioned in the Bible is in the story of the children of Israel's dramatic exodus from Egypt. Let's read together:

So Moses and Aaron came in to Pharaoh and said to him, "Thus says the Lord God of the Hebrews: 'How long will you refuse to humble yourself before Me? Let My people go, that they may serve Me.'"
Exodus 10:3, 4 (NKJV)

One Hebrew word for humble is: עָנָה `anah
It means to bow yourself down, to depress yourself to stoop or to make yourself low.

The primary function of the word "humble" has to do with you lowering yourself in attitude and corresponding action.

Now the reason I want you to see the original Hebrew context and meaning is so we can glean and learn about what humble is and not just what it isn't. The primary function of the word "humble" has to do with you lowering yourself in attitude and corresponding action. It's an intentional choice to make yourself lower not because you're insignificant but because you trust in a God who promised to always lift up those who would humble themselves.

So any time we talk about humble and humility, we're always going to be talking about a willful and intentional decision to make yourself lower in expectation of going higher at a later time or setting. God delights in the hope and expectation that comes from putting your trust in him and not your own self.

The humble principle is this:

Power is never in my own ability but in God's strength that comes by lowering and humbling myself, intentionally making room for grace.

Many people believe they are to make themselves lower expecting nothing in return. I will show you how this is unbiblical and will later turn into false humility, which is actually a form of pride. This is one of the most common ways humble is misunderstood. Now this is why the book is called Upside of Down: How Intentionally Going Lower Can Take You Higher.

So let's dig a little deeper and hopefully develop a working definition of humble that is truly biblical. We've now established that humble people make their own selves lower; they stoop and bow down and make themselves low. But whom should they stoop to?

My humility is always before God, even though at times it will look like I'm making myself low in the presence of people.

Are we telling people to stoop and lower themselves before their bosses? Should they bow before an elected official or a teacher? I believe the biblical context of humble isn't a physical bowing before a person but a spiritual choice to allow someone and something bigger to work on your behalf when you truly live in the power and promises given to the humble.

So in reality, my humility is always before God, even though at times it will look like I'm making myself low in the presence of people. I will show you this in detail when we look at Jesus's teachings on humble, but for now, I want you to realize that being humble is a choice that you must make for yourself.

When you choose humble, you are choosing to make yourself lower to God with the expectation of a hidden power being released because of your humility before God. So a working definition of humble could look something like this:

Humble means to make yourself low before God now, in the certainty that God will exalt you sometime in the future.

Have you ever heard Kim Klement sing the prophetic song, "I am someplace in the future and I look much better than I do right now"? He must have been talking about those who live in the power of humble.

So when you live and operate in the power of humble, you never have to lift yourself or make something happen. Instead, you make room for God to work by always making yourself lower, knowing God will work, and seeing that you will eventually be going higher. Again, let me say that God isn't against you going higher. In fact, he wants to increase your greatness and influence more than you want it. The difference is how you get there. In our studies of humble people, take a look and listen to this and please learn from people like David whom I believe learned how to live in the power of humble. Watch and see the upside of down in action!

My soul shall make its boast in the Lord; The humble shall hear of it and be glad.
Psalm 34:2 (NKJV)

As I write and think about this scripture, I'm thinking about the commercial on television where someone is talking on the phone and moving from place to place, saying, "Can you hear me now?" Have you ever felt like you wish you could hear God better? Have you ever prayed and wished you could hear an answer from God at all? I know I have. Please open your heart to learn a secret and key to hearing God from King David who said, "The humble shall hear." This one scripture is filled with revelation about the humble. The first might be obvious but still must be stated. Humble people boast in the Lord, not themselves!

"Humble means to make yourself low before God now, in the certainty that God will exalt you sometime in the future,"

Now with our working definition of humble and what we have learned so far, we can see some specific attributes of humble. Remember our definition of humble? "Humble means to make yourself low before God now, in the certainty that God will exalt you sometime in the future," and the humble principle is: "Power is never in my own ability, but in God's strength that comes by lowering and humbling myself, intentionally making room for grace."

As you read, I hope you are noticing that a humble person boasts or brags about God's abilities, not their own abilities. It doesn't mean the humble person is weak or doesn't have any abilities but that they choose to rest in God's strength and might rather than their own power. This psalmist known as David, the sweet psalmist of Israel, has been on the run from Saul and it is believed he penned this psalm after pretending to be a mad man in front of the king of Gath. Let's read the story together.

So David escaped from Saul and went to King Achish of Gath But the officers of Achish were unhappy about his being there. "Isn't this David, the king of the land?" they asked. "Isn't he the one the people honor with dances, singing, 'Saul has killed his thousands, and David his ten thousands'?" David heard these comments and was very afraid of what King Achish of Gath might do to him. So he pretended to be insane, scratching on doors and drool- ing down his beard. Finally, King Achish said to his men, "Must you bring me a madman? We already have enough of them around here! Why should I let someone like this be my guest?" 1 Samuel 21:10–15 (NLT)

Now David had, as a young teenage boy, already killed the giant that came from Gath named Goliath. You probably know the story. Now David lowers himself in front of the king pretending to be a madman so he can have some kind of refuge from the pursuit of Saul. David's reputation as a warrior had already come before the king, and David didn't have to boast about what he had done because they already heard it. Now what David did is a very unlikely and extremely humble. Instead of David showing his power, his ability, and his strength, David made himself lower before the king. Now also remember that our definition of humble says we'll make ourselves lower before God, but it might look like we're doing it before men to the naked eye. I believe when you can humble yourself in the same spirit that David did, you haven't postured yourself in weakness but in strength. No future anointed king today with the reputation of greatness would be likely to be so humble. Yet David wasn't actually bowing before a king, but rather his God. David had to trust in God as he humbled himself so that God would affirm and bring to pass the anointing and the words of the prophet Samuel who many years earlier had declared David the true king of Israel, the man after God's heart. How could David, the chosen, beloved man make himself stoop and lower himself? Because he knew eventually God could do what no man could do! David knew that neither Saul nor this Philistine king could keep him from the place God would exalt him to eventually (by the way that's the part we don't like, we all want the exalting now). Let's read what David penned after this encounter with King Achish.

When David penned Psalm 34, he sang about boasting in the Lord and said, "The humble shall hear and be glad." The words "of it" are italicized because they aren't in the original Hebrew text. The translators usually add words that help us understand the text, but sometimes it actually leads us away from what the Lord wanted us to get. In the Hebrew the word for "hear" is the word שמע "*shama,*" which means to *"listen, to hear, to obey and follow."* This word "*shama*" is also found in the verse that Jesus said is part of the greatest of all commandments.

Then one of the scribes came, and having heard them reasoning together, perceiving that he had answered them well, asked him, "Which is the first commandment of all?" Jesus answered him, "The first of all the commandments is: 'Hear, (שמע "**shama**") O Israel, the Lord our God, the Lord is one. And you shall love the Lord your God with all your heart, with all your soul, with all your mind, and with all your strength.' This is the first commandment. And the second, like it, is this: 'You shall love your neighbor as yourself.' There is no other commandment greater than these" (Mark 12:28–31, NKJV).

Jesus answered the question of what is the first and greatest commandment was to "*shama*" (hear). Many people miss the powerful teaching Jesus is giving the scribe. We think Jesus just tells him, "Hey, just put God first," but there is something so much deeper for us to receive from Jesus's teaching. The plain truth is that no one can put God first without prefaced by a heart filled with the willingness to *shama* (hear). In fact, if you ask a Jewish person what's the most holy and important scripture, they will tell you it's Deuteronomy 6:4, and they simply call it **"The Shama"**. But even most Jewish people focus on the latter part of that verse, which declares that God alone is the one and true God. Most teaching and emphasis doesn't focus on the actual word in the Hebrew about listening, hearing, obeying, and following, which is wrapped up in this powerful Hebrew word "shama."

Jesus is quoting form Deuteronomy 6:4 when he says the most important commandment is to: שמע "shama." שמע in Hebrew is transliterated as "shama"—to listen, to hear, to obey, and follow.

There's a powerful verse that's in Isaiah about how the "shama" will actually guide your life if you will listen.

If you wander off the road to the right or the left, you will hear (*shama*) his voice behind you saying, "Here is the road. Follow it." You will take your idols plated with silver and your idols covered with gold, and will throw them away like filth, shouting, "Out of my sight!" Whenever you plant your crops, the Lord will send rain to make them grow and will give you a rich harvest, and your livestock will have plenty of pasture. Isaiah 30:21–23 (GNT)

This passage of scripture in Isaiah gives us insight to what will happen when you truly *shama*. You will hear the voice of the Lord guiding your ears in the direction that gives such clarity as to say "this is the way walk like this." It's like a GPS device would be guiding your life step by step and giving you new strength to now put away anything that would try to lead you astray in your journey such as any idols or uncleanness in this scripture. Then God promises immediately following that there would be the blessing of rain as you continued to listen, hear, obey and follow the voice guiding you. That's what shama is all about.

The promise of God's guidance is a truth that's marked in the lives of those who have learned the secret and key to living in a place where humility allows them to listen and follow God. The promise found in Isaiah is even more powerful because this is an Old Testament promise before the Holy Spirit was given to dwell in believers. Jesus in fact foretold of one of the ministries and missions of the Holy Spirit.

However, when He, the Spirit of truth, has come, He will guide you into all truth; for He will not speak on His own authority, but whatever He hears He will speak; and He will tell you things to come. John 16:13 (NKJV)

Do you see that the Holy Spirit is the one that will cause the humble to *shama* what the Lord Jesus wants to speak in order for you to be led in a certain path or direction? Without the voice of the Holy Spirit speaking in our spiritual ears, we're left to follow what we see with our natural eyes rather than the voice of God that wants to guide us whenever and wherever he desires us to go. The Holy Spirit is God. The Holy Spirit only leads us in truth and in line with the Word of God. One powerful thing I've come to realize is that God always has a plan and it's always better than my own. Now, I'm sure you can remember times in your life when you felt a nudge or pull in a certain direction but didn't yield to it. Afterward you probably said, "Why didn't I listen to that voice?" We're all on a journey of walking and learning how to live and walk in the spirit. There will be times when, instead, we'll walk after the flesh and not do the things we know are right. I just can't wait to ask the great Apostle Paul about this passage:

But I need something more! For if I know the law but still can't keep it, and if the power of sin within me keeps sabotaging my best intentions, I obviously need help! I realize that I don't have what it takes. I can will it, but I can't do it. I decide to do good, but I don't really do it; I decide not to do bad, but then I do it anyway. My decisions, such as they are, don't result in actions. Something has gone wrong deep within me and gets the better of me every time. Romans 7:17–20 (MESSAGE)

Sometimes the most frustrating part of the Christian life is the times when we fail to yield to the voice we know is God and then suffering the dire consequences. Of course, many times the fruit of our not yielding isn't always immediately evident, but it's also true that sometimes in our learning how to be humble and hear we also don't see the fruit as quickly as we'd like. I want you to get this truth deep down in your heart that, even though you don't see the benefit of humble right away, I can assure you it will pay off big time in the future. Let me put this in a way I believe you can really understand. They have done studies on people who are on their way out of this life and no one has ever said, "I regret the time I spent with God or living my life generously or like the Bible teaches." No one ever will regret spending time in God's presence or living full of God's love. Do you think David regretted those nights in God's presence taking care of his father's sheep? Do you think David would have regretted those hours before the Ark worshipping, dancing and singing about his God? The answer is a resounding no! When we get to glory, we will never regret the times lost in God's presence, worshiping or even laying before the Lord. What we probably will all regret is not fully listening, obeying, and following God's unction and leadings in our lives. I don't know about you, but I want to live a life of no regrets. I want to live in the power of humble because the humble hears, the humble listens, the humble follows and obeys the voice of God. I believe as you read this book you will grow in your ability to hear God's voice. Remember the promise to hear is given to the one who is humble.

The scriptures tell an interesting story about a prophet of Israel that confronted the false gods of his day, this prophet was actually dealing with God's people who had not been following, obeying, listening, or hearing God; in fact, they were actually doing the opposite!

So Ahab summoned all the people of Israel and the prophets to Mount Carmel. Then Elijah stood in front of them and said, "How much longer will you waver, hobbling between two opinions? If the Lord is God, follow him! But if Baal is God, then follow him!" But the people were completely silent. Then Elijah said to them, "I am the only prophet of the Lord who is left, but Baal has 450 prophets. Now bring two bulls. The prophets of Baal may choose whichever one they wish and cut it into pieces and lay it on the wood of their altar, but without setting fire to it. I will prepare the other bull and lay it on the wood on the altar, but not set fire to it. Then call on the name of your god, and I will call on the name of the Lord. The god who answers by setting fire to the wood is the true God!" And all the people agreed (1 Kings 18:20–24, NKJV).

The people were in agreement that it was time for one god to be followed. The only problem was that they had never heard God for themselves, but Elijah had heard God, and he was ready to *shama* at any cost. Let's continue with the passage:

At the usual time for offering the evening sacrifice, Elijah the prophet walked up to the altar and prayed, "O Lord, God

of Abraham, Isaac, and Jacob, prove today that you are God in Israel and that I am your servant. Prove that I have done all this at your command. O Lord, answer me! Answer me so these people will know that you, O Lord, are God and that you have brought them back to yourself." Immediately the fire of the Lord flashed down from heaven and burned up the young bull, the wood, the stones, and the dust. It even licked up all the water in the trench! And when all the people saw it, they fell face down on the ground and cried out, "The Lord—he is God! Yes, the Lord is God!"
1 Kings 18:36–39 (NLT)

Did you catch the quote of Elijah? "Prove that I have done all this at your command." Elijah, because he had humbled himself, made room to *shama* God's voice. Elijah heard what no one else had heard. This is what happens when you and I humble ourselves; we hear from God!

Because Elijah heard God's voice and acted on it, the nation of Israel began to turn back to the true God. But do you know that immediately after that Elijah runs in fear because of the threatening of Jezebel, the king's wife? Elijah flees and finds himself in a cave where the word of the Lord comes to him and asks him, "What are you doing here Elijah?" (1 Kings 18:9). After spending the night in a cave, God comes to him finally as "a still, small voice." It's that still, small voice that gives Elijah his mandate and mission if he's going to con- tinue as God's prophet. Now Elijah hears the still, small voice and the instruction that God gives, but like many of us, he has selective listening, only does one of the instructions God gives him, and was not completely obedient to God. This is an example of how not to be. If we're to be humble and *shama*, then we can't just obey and follow what's convenient or some- thing we agree with at the time. Many times we will find it difficult to be humble. Now thankfully Elisha, who was the protégé of Elijah, actually was the one who completed the instructions that God had given his master.

Now let's go back to our Psalm 34 and look at what David is saying in a new light. David says, "I will boast in the Lord and the humble shall *shama*." What is David, the anointed psalmist really saying? He's penning a psalm about a principle that has ruled his life since he was a child keeping his father's sheep that humble people hear, humble people listen, humble people obey, and humble people follow what God says!

When you and I humble ourselves; we hear from God!

The ability to hear God is huge and yet mostly overlooked when it comes to the humble. This is a powerful truth about being humble, and without getting this, we cannot move on. Did you know that when The ability to hear God is huge and yet mostly overlooked when it comes to the humble.

When you're humble, you have the ability to truly hear God speak to you? David is saying that the *shama* belongs to the humble. If you operate in *shama,* you'll have open ears to hear, listen, obey, and follow what God desires for you. Have you ever said, "I wish God would just answer my question"? Or have you come into contact with people who say God never talks to them? Could it be that we haven't understood that God speaks so clearly to those who are humble and it's the humble who really hear when God speaks?

Do you know that the first time God told his people to *shama* (hear), the people heard a word and promise from God about living in physical health? That in Exodus 15:26, the Lord said the people who would hear would know Jehovah as their great physician and the healer? Do you realize it takes the humble to *shama* (hear)? It's the humble people that will make room for grace that brings healing and wholeness. The next time God tells the people to shama (hear) is in the book of Deuteronomy 11:13–14, and those who hear will live with the blessing of abundant rain as well as a multiplication of our days like the days of heaven on earth. All I can say is wow! Wow! The like of blessing is freely given by God's grace to those who keep themselves humble enough to hear and receive when God speaks.

Conclusively, the third time is found in Deuteronomy 15:5–6, and God promises those who will *shama* (hear) that they will be blessed by God as to not be borrowers but rather lenders and reign over the nations. I don't know about you but I want to live in humble so I can continually *shama* (hear) what God wants to tell me. It's my opinion that if a person could just hear from God, their life would be changed. Lord, let us be the people that *shama*!
Jesus said:

He who has ears to hear, let him hear!

Matthew 13:9 (NKJV)

It's not only possible but probable that Jesus, speaking in Hebrew, was talking about *shama* when he spoke about hearing God. In fact, Jesus used this statement many times to infer it wasn't the physical ears that weren't in tune or working; it was their spiritual ears and ability to hear the truth of what God wanted to give them that was being hindered by their ears not being opened to what Jesus was teaching. Could Jesus be inferring to what David penned in Psalm 34 about them not being able to hear because they weren't humble? I know you probably never thought how being humble could influence so much and especially our ability to hear the voice of the Holy Spirit or truly hear the Word of God. Let's read now a little more closely and see if we can get a deeper insight from Jesus himself.

Therefore hear the parable of the sower: When anyone hears the word of the kingdom, and does not understand it, then the wicked one comes and snatches away what was sown in his heart. This is he who received seed by the way-side. But he who received the seed on stony places, this is he who hears the word and immediately receives it with joy; yet he has no root in himself, but endures only for a while. For when tribulation or persecution arises because of the word, immediately he stumbles. Now he who received seed among the thorns is he who hears the word, and the cares of this world and the deceitfulness of riches choke the word, and he becomes unfruitful. But he who received seed on the good ground is he who hears the word and understands it, who indeed bears fruit and produces: some a hundredfold, some sixty, some thirty.

Matthew 13:18–23 (NKJV)

Now let's look at the context of what Jesus is teaching on and how important it is to be humble so you can actually hear it. Jesus is teaching on the parable of the sower, which

Jesus explains in great depth the foundational nature of this parable in the book of Mark.

Then Jesus said to them, "If you can't understand the meaning of this parable, how will you understand all the other parables?" (Mark 4:1,3 NLT)

So what is the main subject of this parable? It's all about hearing! Jesus teaches that, even though the power of God's Word will never return void, unless it gets to a heart that will s*hama* and fully hear that word it won't produce fruit. This is why it's so important that you and I learn how to live in the power of humble. This is why David said, "The humble shall hear, the humble shall *shama*!" I am so blown away by this teaching that I'm deeply stirred as I write. As a pastor, I love my sheep but get so discouraged when they won't do what they know they should. Sometimes I think, "Why do I preach my heart out on Sunday when so many of God's people put the hearing of God's Word and corporate worship somewhere lower on the list of priorities than directed?" Now I know I'm venting right now, but it's not that I want people to come and hear me. I want them to live in the power of hearing God and following what he desires for their lives. Jesus's teaching on the parable of the sower proves that people have been the same for thousands of years. God's Word is always waiting and looking to land in the heart of one who will receive it with humility.

I believe that when David humbled himself and acted like a madman in front of that Philistine king, God saw it and took notice. If you don't know the story, I'll give you a quick briefing. David as a young boy was anointed by God to be the next king. The present king Saul was nothing but insecure, proud, and intimidated by the heart and youthfulness of David and how the people lifted David up in song. David never retaliated in any way when King Saul began to try to kill him and turn the people against him. King Saul's pursuit of David drove David to live in the wilderness in fear for his life while never taking the opportunity to kill Saul because he was God's anointed leader. Because David never lifted himself up but continually humbled himself, there was a hidden power released in his life that caused good to come to him in the midst of his trials.

David sang about what he knew, and he knew it was God who would ultimately vindicate him. In 1 Samuel 22 after David leaves King Achish, he goes to the wilderness, and there God releases to him what could only be given to the humble.

David therefore departed from there and escaped to the cave of Adullam. So when his brothers and all his father's house heard it, they went down there to him. And every- one who was in distress, everyone who was in debt, and everyone who was discontented gathered to him. So he became captain over them. And there were about four hundred men with him.
The ability to shama is given to those who are humble!

1 Samuel 22:1–2 (NKJV)

This is the next chapter immediately after David humbles himself with seemingly no immediate results, yet God releases into David's care four hundred who can receive from David's leadership after making himself lower. Look what God does! Now these are the same men who are later known as David's mighty men. They came broken, bruised, misunderstood, and mistreated, and yet with David, they were healed. I like to say in Saul's selfish kingdom these men were misfits, but in David's humble wilderness, they were mighty men. They came in debt, discouraged, and distressed, but with David, they were all abundantly blessed. They came wounded of heart, but with David, they became powerful strong warriors that brought fear to their enemies. What made the difference? David was a man who knew the humble shall shama. David modeled this almost-forgotten quality in leaders today. Can you ever imagine the leader of any nation doing what David did? Of course not! Why? Because most people think they have to boast and lift themselves up and therefore anything they do get is because they have worked for it, manipulated for it or made it happen with their own strength. David was not this kind of leader. David understood that true influence and power is not to be used for selfish gain but to help and lead others higher. David never got to the throne because he pushed himself. In fact, you'll see that God always used others to bring David to prominence. Many of today's leaders are usually boasting in what they've done or accomplished and not boasted in the Lord like David penned in Psalm 42. The ability to shama is given to those who are humble. The humble shall *shama*. This is a powerful and seldom taught truth. I've been around and have heard many boastful people, and I'm sure you have as well. It actually is a turn off, and I would rather be around people who simply hear from God and obey what God tells them to do. I don't like it when someone says, "God has sent me to accomplish or do such and such." If God sends you, just do it and don't boast in yourself or what God is giving you to do. Can you see how we need more of this kind of humble? We need to see people make themselves lower, not lift themselves up and jockey for some kind of position of power. David stayed humble just like when he was young and took care of his father's sheep. No one was watching David while he spent years in the wilderness alone intentionally staying low before his God. When David went on a mission given by his dad to check on his brothers, David used that opportunity to boast in the greatness of God. Listen now to David as he visits his brothers on the battlefield.

"Your servant has killed both lion and bear; and this uncircumcised Philistine will be like one of them, seeing he has defied the armies of the living God." Moreover David said, "The Lord, who delivered me from the paw of the lion and from the paw of the bear, He will deliver me from the hand of this Philistine." 1 Samuel 17: 36–37 (NKJV)

Can you see true biblical humility working in David? David was bold to point to the strength of God working in his life when he was taking care of his father's sheep. David recognized it was God's strength, not his own. He rested in that strength more than once and was now ready to continue to see what God would do through the humble. In fact, I believe this is what separated David so greatly from King Saul, who would later try to tell David that he needs his armor to protect himself from Goliath. David quickly puts off the armor of Saul, having not tested or proved its abilities. What David had seen was a God who could deliver with the simplicity of a sling and a stone. Would you like to be like David who didn't trust in his own abilities but trusted in the strength and might of God? You see, the hidden power in the humble is a genuine trust in the Lord.

His boasting was always in God and not in his own power or ability. David gives us this profound key. "The humble shall hear."

Your ears shall hear a word behind you, saying, "This is the way, walk in it," Whenever you turn to the right hand or whenever you turn to the left.
Isaiah 30:21 (NKJV)

CHAPTER THREE:

What's Killing Today's Church?

I HAD THIS dream that was so vivid and really did something to me. Now before I tell you my dream, I want to give you a biblical truth about dreams and the influence a dream can have in your life. I like to think of dreams as a vision or story that comes from God while we are sleeping. He gives them to us while we sleep so we can receive them without any deter- rents or hindrances. There's something that happens to all of us when we really sleep. You know what I'm talking about, don't you? It's in the sleep state that our minds seem to shut down to the daily grind and we seem to drift into another world or altered state where we believe and can do anything (*you know like fly*). Sometimes I believe God has to speak to us in a dream because we are so distracted and congested with the busyness of life. God sometimes will use a dream to break through into our subconscious while we're sleeping to get a divine message or answer to us.

For God speaks once, or twice, and yet no one listens. In a dream, a special dream of the night, when deep sleep comes upon men, while they sleep in their beds, then He opens the ears of men. He teaches them and makes them afraid telling them of danger, that He may turn man away from wrong-doing and keep him from pride. He keeps his soul from going to the place of the dead. And He keeps his life from being destroyed by the sword." Job 33:14–18 (NLV)

This scripture found in Job gives insight to how God will use dreams while we're sleeping to get a message to us that we might not get any other way. Now I know there might be some of you that don't really give credibility to your dreams, and I'm not saying God is speaking through every dream.   However, I believe when you do have what I like to call a prophetic dream, you should take special heed to what it could be telling you. A dream can warn you; a dream can help to give you guidance and even clarity about something or someone, so please pay attention to your dreams!

Now I had this very vivid dream one night. It was so clear and also quite thought-provoking and downright scary to be quite honest. In this dream, I saw a three-pronged instrument like a pitchfork of some kind and each prong had some wording on them. Now, I also saw what I believe was the devil holding this pitchfork and using it to slay the people of God. Each of the three prongs had a name written, "rebellion, stubbornness, and apathy." In the dream God was showing me the three things that the devil was using to stop the church. I knew God wanted me to see this because I had been also asking God what's going on at our church. God was showing me that in my church the devil was using this three-pronged fork to hinder God's people and the work of the kingdom in their lives. Now also the three-pronged fork had a long stem so it reminded me of a pitchfork. The stem is actually the root of the three prongs of rebellion, stubbornness, and apathy. Do you know what the root of these three prongs is? It's one of the things the Bible says God hates, and it's nothing more than pride. Pride is a root or stem that must be dealt with because it will always bring you down. The scripture says:

Pride precedes a disaster, and an arrogant attitude precedes a fall.
Proverbs 16:18 (GWT)

I can remember this dream, which was so vivid and so real. I can remember feeling so helpless in my dream as I told God I couldn't help these people, because they're full of rebellion, stubbornness, and apathy. Then the Lord told me something that was about to blow my mind. He told me I was going to lead the people out of from the root of pride and away from the rebellion, stubbornness and apathy that I had seen in my dream. As their pastor, God anointed me and in my dream God told me that I had the power to do it. To be quite honest and vulnerable, I felt incapable and completely powerless to do such a task. In fact, as I write this I still feel the same way. Not only did God continue to tell me I was going to lead them out, but he wouldn't relent in letting me know that I was given this task and would complete it. To be honest, I love my church and believe we have some of the most loving and giving Christian people I know. There are so many great things about our church and people that I just wish everyone could come and experience just one service. However, I know when God speaks it's always from a place of love and truth and there's no perfect church. For all churches have good people in them that struggle because the stem of pride always leads to rebellion, stubbornness or apathy. The more I thought about my vivid dream and the words that I believe God was speaking, I began to see that the church as a whole has largely been plagued with this three-pronged pitchfork, the root being a spirit of pride that gives birth to rebellion, stubbornness, and apathy. Perhaps even this book Upside of Down, God can use to be a step and help in leading God's people out of these deadly traps of the devil. Now the Bible says:

So that we may not be exploited by Satan (for we are not ignorant of his schemes).
2 Corinthians 2:11 (NET BIBLE)

The Bible is clear that Christians shouldn't live in ignorance to the schemes and tactics that the devil would try to employ to stop the work of God in our lives, in our families, churches, and our respective heritage, cultures, and nations. What I am about to talk about is not new, but for some reason, we can get blind or used to deception and not recognize it for what it really is. You see, you can attempt to coddle a snake or a wild animal, but sooner or later, it will bite and try to devour because that's what they are and what they do by nature. The Bible says:

Those who call evil good and good evil are as good as dead, who turn darkness into light and light into darkness, who turn bitter into sweet and sweet into bitter.
Isaiah 5:20 (NET BIBLE)

There's nothing good about pride, rebellion, stubbornness, or apathy. For the root of pride has been used by Satan to bring many to a place of ruin. When someone is prideful, I like to say that they are already full and now have no room for what God wants to do. When we allow the root of pride to dominate our thinking, our future becomes cloudy and dark. God will always resist the proud. He can't help those who say they're already full. Pride will always birth a spirit of rebellion, stubbornness, and apathy. These things are never touted as good or something we should aspire to in the Bible. Jesus himself warned Peter before his denial of the Lord in this scripture:

And the Lord said, "Simon, Simon! Indeed, Satan has asked for you, that he may sift you as wheat. But I have prayed for you, that your faith should not fail; and when you have returned to Me, strengthen your brethren." But he said to Him, "Lord, I am ready to go with You, both to prison and to death." Then He said, "I tell you, Peter, the rooster shall not crow this day before you will deny three times that you know Me" (Luke 22:31–34, NKJV).

Jesus knew that Satan wanted to have Peter and all the disciples. Peter was so full of pride and confident in his own abilities that he boasted and told the Lord that he was ready, not just to go to prison and to death, but to go with Jesus wherever the road would lead. Now here we find some powerful truths we can glean. First we find that Jesus already knows that the enemy desires to have us. In the Greek, it is the word **exaiteō**: *"it means to demand that one be given over to the power of another for torture or punishment."* This is what the enemy wanted to do to the disciples and specifically Peter. Jesus here says to Peter, "I have already prayed and seen your conversion and what you'll do afterwards for my kingdom. Peter, you'll be one who will strengthen the church." But before Peter does, he'll have to deal with the proud and arrogant heart he has. Peter will later weep bitterly in repentance because of his denial of the One whom God revealed to Peter as the Son of God.

A dream can warn you; a dream can help to give you guidance and even clarity about something or someone, so please pay attention to your dreams!

"When Jesus came into the region of Caesarea Philippi, He asked His disciples, saying, "Who do men say that I, the Son of Man, am?" So they said, "Some say John the Baptist, some Elijah, and others Jeremiah or one of the prophets." He said to them, "But who do you say that I am?" Simon Peter answered and said, "You are the Christ, the Son of the living God." Jesus answered and said to him, "Blessed are you, Simon Bar-Jonah, for flesh and blood has not revealed this to you, but My Father who is in heaven.

And I also say to you that you are Peter, and on this rock I will build My church, and the gates of Hades shall not prevail against it. And I will give you the keys of the kingdom of heaven, and whatever you bind on earth will be bound in heaven, and whatever you loose on earth will be loosed in heaven." Matthew 16:13–19 (NKJV)

Do you know that you can have God speak to you and still be filled with pride? Now remember the opposite and antithesis of humble is pride, and it's the only thing that

God's grace will resist. So I hope you see how imperative it is that we see pride for what it is, a deadly device that will devour us from the inside out.

The three-pronged pitchfork that I saw the devil wielding was a long stem of pride, leading to three prongs of rebellion, stubbornness, and apathy. This is how they manifest them- selves and speak:

- **Rebellion says, "I won't obey!"**
- **Stubbornness says, "I won't hear!"**
- **Apathy says, "I won't move!"**

Can you see what's common in all of these? It's the words "I won't!" It's not that they can't or don't have the ability; it's the arrogance and refusal to do anything but what "I" choose. The root or stem is pride, which lifts itself up and says it's already full and self-sufficient and refuses to be humble. This is why I believe it is so important to be intentional in going lower and not allowing pride in any form to cause you to lift yourself up. Remember the upside of down is that when you intentionally make yourself lower it is God and grace that will take you higher.

This is dangerous ground because pride comes from the spirit of antichrist, which always uses the prefix, "I" in a way that is self-exalting and selfish. It's not the heart of the humble person but the one who feels the need to boast in them- selves rather than God. The three-pronged pitchfork of rebel- lion, stubbornness, and apathy can only be defeated when the root of pride gives way to a humble heart that will *shama* God. After all, the greatest commandment in the Bible starts with *shama* because when we hear and follow God, we unconsciously yield to His will and live dependent rather than like pride, independent of God. ***Rebellion says, "I won't obey!" Stubbornness says, "I won't hear!" Apathy says, "I won't move!"***

Now let's look at the story of King Saul who had a natural inclination to be proud, possibly because he was a head taller that the rest of the Israelites. Now the Bible says that the prophet Samuel came and confronted his disobedience when it came to completely destroy the Amalekites. So Samuel said, "When you were little in your own eyes, were you not head of the tribes of Israel? And did not the Lord anoint you king over Israel?" (1 Samuel 15:17, NKJV)

How amazing is this king who started out small in his own eyes. Would you say that was a humble man? I believe like many of us, we start out with the right heart but don't keep the right heart when we start getting successful. Saul is so much like us today. When Saul was humble, God exalted him and made him the first king of Israel. What an honor and privilege! It didn't take long for Saul to forget his humility and begin to operate in pride, not wanting to lose his position and authority. In fact, I would venture to say to anyone who reads this book please don't let pride keep you from being tender, soft, and pliable before God. Sometimes it's good to remember your humble beginnings and continue to go back to those early days when you knew, unless God exalted and helped, you really wouldn't have or be anything. Now Samuel is the prophet or seer. God has revealed to him the heart of Saul and how Saul is now full of pride and won't change! Even when confronted by the prophet, Saul makes excuses and doesn't do what's commanded of him.

"And the Lord sent you on a mission and told you, 'Go and completely destroy the sinners, the Amalekites, until they are all dead.' Why haven't you obeyed the Lord? Why did you rush for the plunder and do what was evil in the Lord's sight?" "But I did obey the Lord," Saul insisted. "I carried out the mission he gave me. I brought back King Agag, but I destroyed everyone else. Then my troops brought in the best of the sheep, goats, cattle, and plunder to sacrifice to the Lord your God in Gilgal." But Samuel replied, "What is more pleasing to the Lord: your burnt offerings and sacrifices or your obedience to his voice? Listen! Obedience is better than sacrifice, and submission is better than offering the fat of rams. Stubbornness as bad as worshiping idols. So because you have rejected the command of the Lord, he has rejected you as king." 1 Samuel 15:18–23 (NLT)

Now I want you to remember that rebellion says, "I won't obey," and stubbornness says, "I won't hear." It's these two sins that Saul was willfully committing, and God couldn't give grace while rebellion and stubbornness prevailed in Saul's heart.

The root or stem of Saul's rebellion and stubbornness was the spirit of pride, which Saul had in abundance; possibly because he was full of secret insecurities, trust issues, and self- pity. Now at the end of the day, it isn't important why we have pride but how we deal with it. For if left unrequited, pride will always bring us down. I want you to think of pride as trusting and relying in your own strength and ability. Pride always lifts "self " up instead of lifting up God or his Word.

These six things the Lord hates, Yes, seven are an abomination to Him: A proud look. Proverbs 6:16, 17A (NKJV)

The first on the list of the things God hates is not just pride but literally a prideful eye! Let me give you a few more scriptures on how dangerous and detrimental pride is.

The Lord tears down the house of the proud, but he protects the property of widows.
Proverbs 15:25 (NLT) You rebuke the proud—the cursed, who stray from Your commandments.

Psalm 119:21 (NKJV) Haughty eyes, a proud heart, and evil actions are all sin.

Proverbs 21:4 (NLT) Pride goes before destruction, and haughtiness before a fall.

Proverbs, 16:18 (NLT)

Pride ends in humiliation, while humility brings honor.

Proverbs 29:23 (NLT)

I want you to think of pride as trusting and relying in your own strength and ability.

The plain and simple truth is that pride is never, never a good thing. It can only lead you down. Another example of pride is found in the book of Daniel about a King who lifted himself up rather than God. Now all of this happened to King Nebuchadnezzar. After twelve months, he happened to be walking around on the battlements of the royal palace of Babylon. The king uttered these words: "Is this not the great Babylon that I have built for a royal residence by my own mighty strength and for my majestic honor?" While these words were still on the king's lips, a voice came down from heaven: "It is hereby announced to you, King Nebuchadnezzar, that your kingdom has been removed from you! You will be driven from human society, and you will live with the wild animals. You will be fed grass like oxen, and seven periods of time will pass by for you before you understand that the Most High is ruler over human kingdoms and gives them to whomever he wishes." (Daniel 4:28– 32, NET BIBLE)

The king was full of pride and didn't realize that what he had received as a king wasn't because of his great abilities or strength but rather in the God who allowed him to enjoy and wield the power and authority that was given to him by God alone. In the midst of his personal boasting, the prophetic dream that he had been given now came to pass and it would take seven years for his pride to leave him.

Let's read on:
At that time my sanity returned to me. I was restored to the honor of my kingdom, and my splendor returned to me. My ministers and my nobles were seeking me out, and I was reinstated over my kingdom. I became even greater than before. Now I, Nebuchadnezzar, praise and exalt and glorify the King of heaven, for all his deeds are right and his ways are just. He is able to bring down those who live in pride. Daniel 4:36–37 (NET BIBLE)

After those seven years, the king recognized the King of heaven, the one who freely gave him what he had received and now lived in light of that newfound knowledge. Unfortunately, his son later didn't learn from his father's repentance and humility.

Your majesty, the Most High God gave Nebuchadnezzar your father the kingdom, as well as greatness, glory and majesty. Because of the greatness he gave him, all the peoples, nations and languages trembled with fear before him. Anyone he wanted to, he put to death; anyone he wanted to, he kept alive; anyone he wanted to, he advanced; and anyone he wanted to, he humbled. But when he grew proud and his spirit became hard, he began treating people arrogantly, so he was deposed from his royal throne, and his glory was taken away from him. He was driven from human society, his heart was made like that of an animal, he lived with the wild donkeys, he was fed with grass like an ox, and his body was drenched with dew from the sky; until he learned that the Most High God rules in the human kingdom and sets up over it whomever he pleases. But, Belshazzar, you, his son, have not humbled your heart, even though you knew all this. Instead, you have exalted yourself against the Lord of heaven by having them bring you the vessels from his house; and you and your lords, your wives and your concubines drank wine from them; then you offered praise to your gods of silver, gold, bronze, iron, wood and stone, which can't see, hear or know anything. Meanwhile, God, who holds your very breath in his hands, and to whom belongs everything you do, you have not glorified.
Daniel 5:18–23 (CJB)

We need not be like Belshazzar who didn't learn from the life of his father. We should listen to the warnings of scripture and not allow pride in any form in our lives. In fact, when pride comes, it will usually be joined by rebellion so we won't obey and stubbornness that causes us not to listen to the very instruction we need that will bring our freedom. When Jesus came to his people, they refused to listen and follow him. They were stubborn and this caused the people whom he came for to miss out on their time of visitation. I definitely don't want to miss out on what Jesus has for me. How about you?

Then Jesus said to those Jews who believed Him, "If you abide in My word, you are My disciples indeed. And you shall know the truth, and the truth shall make you free." John 8:31–32 (NKJV)

I know that you are Abraham's descendants, but you seek to kill Me, because My word has no place in you. I speak what I have seen with My Father, and you do what you have seen with your father. John 8:37–38 (NKJV)

He who is of God hears God's words; therefore you do not hear, because you are not of God. John 8:47 (KJV)

Now in these scriptures, Jesus is talking to people who are Jews and are supposed to be meditating on the Word, living and breathing God's Word. Now Jesus is more than the writ- ten Word; he is the Living Word who is right in front of them speaking to them about hearing and abiding in the word of truth. The people have natural ears to hear, but their hearts are shut. They are refusing to hear and are filled with stubborn- ness. This is what happens to many good Christians today. Many times truth will come to us in a different form than we are used to. Like Jesus who came as the living Word to people, they didn't receive Jesus even though he was the author of the written Word himself.

Stubborn people are so hard to get through to, and that's why I felt so helpless when God gave me the dream, which put stubbornness as the center prong in the devil's pitchfork. One of the things that I hate to do is to argue with people. I confess, I'm not one who likes to bicker back and forth try-ing to get my opinion or my point of view heard. I'm that way because I know that when someone has refused to hear, it's no use trying to convince him or her with human argu-ments. That's why I felt so discouraged as a preacher of God's Word, frustrated that my people, whom I love and care about, were not even able to hear a word of freedom because of that stubbornness.

Please look at these scriptures about stubbornness:

That the generation to come might know them, The children who would be born, That they may arise and declare them to their children, That they may set their hope in God, And not forget the works of God, But keep His commandments; And may not be like their fathers, A stubborn and rebellious generation, A generation that did not set
its heart aright, And whose spirit was not faithful to God.
Psalm 78:6–8, (NKJV)

But when the judge died, the people went right back to their old ways—but even worse than their parents! —

running after other gods, serving and worshiping them. Stubborn as mules, they didn't drop a single evil practice.

Judges 2:19 (MESSAGE)

Your ancestors refused to listen to this message. They stubbornly turned away and put their fingers in their ears to keep from hearing. They made their hearts as hard as stone, so they could not hear the instructions or the messages that the Lord of Heaven's Armies had sent them by his Spirit through the earlier prophets. That is why the Lord of Heaven's Armies was so angry with them.
Zechariah 7:11–12 (NLT)

A story about another very stubborn man is Jonah, who didn't want to hear and obey the word of the Lord about going to preach to Nineveh. We know how Jonah, after being swallowed by a great fish, goes and does finally preach. Also, what he had previously anticipated happened to Jonah's great distress. I think Jonah might have also had his stubbornness quite possibly rooted in pride because it seems he wants to place himself above God's righteous or merciful judgments concerning Nineveh when God decided to spare the destruction of that country. When the people repented, Jonah got beyond mad and he became infuriated!

But it displeased Jonah exceedingly, and he became angry. So he prayed to the Lord, and said, "Ah, Lord, was not this what I said when I was still in my country? Therefore I fled previously to Tarshish; for I know that You are a gracious and merciful God, slow to anger and abundant in lovingkindness, One who relents from doing harm. Therefore now, O Lord, please take my life from me, for it

is better for me to die than to live!" Then the Lord said, "Is it right for you to be angry?"
(Jonah 4:1–4, NKJV).

We must be careful not to be stubborn and not hear what God asks of us even if we don't like what God is asking or the results it might bring. The stubborn heart is a refusal to hear and a very dangerous place to be. It is also a stubborn heart that is compared to an idol, which has no ability to hear, answer or respond to its worshipper.

Whoever stubbornly refuses to accept criticism will suddenly be destroyed beyond recovery.
Proverbs 29:1 (NLT)

Finally, allow me to deal with the third prong of apathy.

Therefore, to him who knows to do good and does not do it, to him it is sin. James 4:17 (NKJV)

Apathy is defined as:

1.   *Lack of interest or concern, especially regarding matters of general importance or appeal; indifference.*
2.   *Lack of emotion or feeling; impassiveness.*

The spiritual, emotional, and physical disconnection to things of great importance describes many. One of the phenomena of our day and studies support how, even in life and death situations, many won't stop and help one who could be rescued with some effort. How's that for apathy? You see, it's not that the ability is lacking, but the passion to move past what's comfortable and convenient. The scary thing to me is that, what starts out as apathy and the refusal to move, later turns into the inability to move because, like a body part that doesn't get used, its strength and muscles can deteriorate to the point that it can't move. This is, in fact, what worried me about the dream I had. In the dream, the devil used apathy to cause the strength of God's people to deteriorate to the point that they couldn't rise up and fight! Let me give you an example of this.

If you're a church person, you know that all churches have a need for people to get involved and help in the work. This is true of all churches no matter how large or small. Have you heard the about the 20/80 principle? It means that 20 percent do all the work, while the other 80 percent get the benefits. Why is this? This principle isn't just in church; it's everywhere you look. For the most part the work is done by a few, while the 80 percent majority is apathetic and it seems no matter what or who pleas for their help, they refuse to move in spite of what may be urgently needed. Now remember that the person with apathy says, "I won't move!" It's not that they can't move but refuse to do what they know is right. This is what James describes as a person who knows to do something but refuses to move and do it. This is not only wrong, but according to James is a willful sin. Now this attitude is one that comes with some disturbing trends. For once a person refuses to move, they become dry, and the lack of use causes the elasticity of spiritual muscles to deteriorate. I believe the apathy can give way to another condition known as:

Atrophy: n. pl. at·ro·phies

1.   *Pathology A wasting or decrease in size of a body organ, tissue, or part owing to disease, injury, or lack of use: muscular atrophy of a person affected with paralysis.*

2.   *A wasting away, deterioration, or diminution: intellectual atrophy.*
v.   at·ro·phied, at·ro·phy·ing, at·ro·phies
v.tr. To cause to wither or deteriorate; affect with atrophy.
v.intr. To waste away; wither or deteriorate.

Atrophy occurs according to the definition of a wasting away or deterioration due to lack of use. It reminds me of the man with the withered hand whom, because of lack of moisture and use, all future use of the arm would be impossible except through a miracle from Jesus. The scripture teaches in Luke 6 that this man's right hand was, in the Greek:

xēros 1) dry
a.   *Of members of the body deprived of their natural juices, shrunk, wasted, withered*
b.   *Of the land in distinction from the water*

Tradition says that this man was a mason and needed his dominant right hand to lay the bricks and build. The right hand hadn't been used in so long that it was impossible for him to do what Jesus commanded.

Now it happened on another Sabbath, also, that He entered the synagogue and taught. And a man was there whose right hand was withered. So the scribes and Pharisees watched Him closely, whether He would heal on the Sabbath, that

they might find an accusation against Him. But He knew their thoughts, and said to the man who had the withered hand, "Arise and stand here." And he arose and stood. Then Jesus said to them, "I will ask you one thing: Is it lawful on the Sabbath to do good or to do evil, to save life or to destroy?" And when He had looked around at them all, He said to the man, "Stretch out your hand." And he did so, and his hand was restored as whole as the other.
Luke 6: 6–10 (NKJV)

Jesus was asking this man to stretch what he could not do. Because of the lack of moisture, his arm was now nothing more than a dried up piece of leathery skin and bones. This is a picture of what happens when we don't allow the water and moisture of God's Word to flow in our lives when we aren't doing what we know as Christians we should do. This apathy, now kicked up to another level will manifest itself as atrophy, and has become acceptable in Christendom. We no longer hold people accountable for their lack of activity and obedience and we accept it as normal behavior and the way church has become. This is actually the sin of omission. "Remember, it is sin to know what you ought to do and then not do it."

James 4:17 (NLT) Today, no one will probably confront this type of sin, but it's as serious as sin can be.

It's also teaching by example to the next generation that it's "normal" to be lukewarm. Yet Jesus said it was that kind of follower He would be forced to "vomit." Revelation 3:16 (NKJV)

What the Lord showed me about the three-pronged pitch-fork of the devil was that it was rebellion, stubbornness, and apathy over the stem of pride that was robbing the church of her effectiveness and mission to go and make disciples of all nations. The church has, for many, been nothing more than a place of sleep while in the midst of a great potential harvest. We cannot afford to be asleep with apathy now.

The one who gathers crops in the summer is a wise son, but the one who sleeps during the harvest is a son who brings shame to himself." Proverbs 10:6 (NET BIBLE)

The heart of the Heavenly Father has always been for the multiplication of God's family. Yet in the midst of many promises of revival and salvation of the world we see a real enemy working on keeping the church in a state of apathy, never exercising her spiritual muscles and use the power she has been graciously given for this hour.
Maybe this is why Jesus said:

The harvest is great, but the workers are few. So pray to the Lord who is in charge of the harvest; ask him to send more workers into his fields.
Matthew 9:37–38 (NLT)

Could it be that the Lord already knows how apathetic his people have become? What could change this? God, can you please show me how I can lead your people out of apathy? Perhaps the "leading out of apathy" is to first realize that the best part of the church might be asleep and need to be awaked.

Proclaim this among the nations: "Prepare for war! Wake up the mighty men, Let all the men of war draw near, Let them come up. Beat your plowshares into swords And your pruning hooks into spears; Let the weak say, 'I am strong.' "Assemble and come, all you nations, And gather together all around. Cause Your mighty ones to go down there, O Lord. "Let the nations be wakened, and come up to the Valley of Jehoshaphat; For there I will sit to judge all the surrounding nations. Put in the sickle, for the harvest is ripe. Joel 3:9–13a (NKJV)

Please join me as we wake up the church and bring her back to live in the power of humble and say no more to what is killing us! Say no to the three-pronged pitchfork of hell and remember what the enemy really wants us to say and believe:

- **Rebellion says, "I won't obey!"**
- **Stubbornness says, "I won't hear!"**
- **Apathy says, "I won't move!"**
- **Pride says, "I'm full!"**

Will you now say with me what the UPside of Down humble heart would say to replace the enemy's lie with truth?

- **My humble heart says, "I will obey!"**
- **My humble mind says, "I will hear!"**
- **My humble will says, "I will move forward!"**
- **My humble life says, "I make room for grace."**

But he gives us even more grace to stand against such evil desires. As the Scriptures say, "God opposes the proud but favors the humble" (James 4:6, NLT).

My humble heart says, "I will obey!" My humble mind says, "I will hear!" My humble will says, "I will move forward!" My humble life says, "I make room for grace."

CHAPTER FOUR:

The Humble Upside of Down Life

T HE PROFOUND, AND I believe hidden, truth is that heaven looks and longs for those who will live in the principle of humble. Again, the humble principle is "Power is never in my own ability, but in God's strength that comes by lowering and humbling myself, intentionally making room for grace."

Let's look at the scriptures and see what the Bible really teaches about humble and also what it does not. There is an idea going around about humility that is not congruent with the teaching in the Bible about humble at it has confused many into what is known as a false humility.

The humble principle is "Power is never in my own ability, but in God's strength that comes by lowering and humbling myself, intentionally making room for grace."

This false humility happens when someone, for their own selfish gain poses as humble, while in actuality loving and desiring the praise or acceptance of those whom they impress by their assumed humble life.

This also gives way to another error in the teaching and misunderstanding of true biblical humility, which doesn't teach the "hating of oneself " or not giving the proper acknowledgement to the gifts and talents that reside in all people as gifts that come from God himself. The Bible clearly teaches that we are all made in God's image and are "fearfully and wonderfully made" (Psalm 139, NKJV).

Check out this translation:
I thank you because I am awesomely made, wonderfully; your works are wonders—I know this very well.
Psalm 139:14 (CJB)

So to hate yourself and call it humble or to not acknowledge the awesomeness of what is in you is not what living humble is about. In truth, the scriptures teach the power of a humble life that is so amazing and powerful that I believe the enemy has tried to hide this revelation in order to keep people living in the dark about how God intends for us to truly live.

An example of this is found in this scripture:

O my people, what have I done to you? What have I done to make you tired of me? Answer me! For I brought you out of Egypt and redeemed you from slavery. I sent Moses, Aaron, and Miriam to help you. Don't you remember, my people, how King Balak of Moab tried to have you cursed and how Balaam son of Beor blessed you instead? And remember your journey from Acacia Grove to Gilgal, when I, the

Lord, did everything I could to teach you about my faithfulness. "What can we bring to the Lord? What kind of offerings should we give him? Should we bow before God with offerings of yearling calves? Should we offer him thousands of rams and ten thousand rivers of olive oil? Should we sacrifice our firstborn children to pay for our sins? No, O people, the Lord has told you what is good, and this is what he requires of you: to do what is right, to love mercy, and to walk humbly with your God.
Micah 6:3–8 (NLT)

The prophet is letting the people know how God had showed them his faithfulness despite the many obstacles and opportunities that had tried to stop them. He talks about the deliverance from Egypt and the bondage of slavery that they had been freed of, and how, after they left Egypt, they were protected from the curse of King Balak and God turned the curse into a blessing. Micah let the people know it wasn't in what you can give to God that makes you right, but that he'll always be faithful to give to you what you need and just requires something small from us. The small thing is found in the last part of the verse when the prophet says God wants you "to do what is right," what you already know you should do when it comes to love and mercy. The scripture ends with a call to truly live by walking humble with God.

I find this interesting because the call to a humble life is a life of adventure, not a boring life. It's life where the fun is. When you can partner with God and give good things to those who don't deserve it and to love is the Hebrew the word: חֶסֶד **checed.** It is actually the loving kindness and grace of God. Here the scripture is teaching that the humble life is one that embraces the qualities and characteristics of a loving and graceful God and then lives these out by walking hand in hand with their Creator. The humble life here isn't one of self-abasement, self-denial, or selfishness. Instead, it's one that acknowledges the possibilities of doing and living in God's heart of doing what's right and gracious while always walking humbly with God. It's in the walking humbly that releases to us what we need to impart to others. As long as we walk humbly, we're making room for God and his grace that we all so desperately need. Now this is just the beginning. Look at this:

If My people who are called by My name will humble themselves, and pray and seek My face, and turn from their wicked ways, then I will hear from heaven, and will forgive their sin and heal their land. Now My eyes will be open and My ears attentive to prayer made in this place.
2 Chronicles 7:14–15 (NKJV)

This scripture is one that's quoted at prayer meetings and whenever we want to emphasize the importance of prayer and reviving of a nation. Because we've always seen this scripture in light of prayer, we might have missed something because of our narrow focus. In this scripture those who bear and are called by the name of God is Israel, for even in the Hebrew name "Israel" is found the letters לֵא **El**, which means God. So Israel, who is marked as a people of God, must do more than just wear that name as a badge of honor but must, as a people, take the position of humble before God. Now as many times as I've read and heard this scripture preached, I must confess for the most part it's been heard with a narrow focus of prayer, seeking God's face and turning from wickedness. But do you see the first part of

75

this prayer is for the called to be humble. In fact, if the first part is not done, could it be possible that all the prayer, seeking God's face and turning away from wickedness, could produce little or no results? Now some of you are thinking, "Come on, Pastor, God hears us when we pray no matter what!" If that is true, why then is it written:

Therefore the Lord said: "In as much as these people draw near with their mouths and honor Me with their lips, but have removed their hearts far from Me, and their fear toward Me is taught by the commandment of men. Isaiah 29:13 (NKJV)

Jesus himself quotes this verse that Isaiah penned in Mathew 15:8 and Mark 7:6.

The truth is many will claim to seek God's face and turn from wickedness, but without humbling themselves and without a humble heart; God will resist them. Now take a look at proverbs teaching:

Surely he mocks the mockers, but he gives grace to the humble Proverbs 3:34, (WEB)

This scripture is the foundation scripture for what James and Peter quote about God resisting the proud and giving grace to the humble. For some reason the church hasn't wanted to live in humble. But what some have failed to understand is that the only way God hears us when we pray is when we humble ourselves first. God is the Creator and Controller of the universe and we think we can come with arrogance and pride before his throne and get heard? Without humility and reverence, we expect our selfish and self-centered agendas to get God's attention. I don't think so! I will tell you what will get God's attention speedily; it'll be the humble heart. When Solomon dedicated the temple the Lord spoke to his people that they must allow the spirit of humble to be the first priority even before they pray, seek his face, or turn from their wicked ways. Today we think being humble is optional, like having a side of mayo or a pickle on a burger. We don't realize, *"No humble no burger!"* (Sorry with the food metaphor. I might be getting a little hungry while writing.) Now let's dig a little deeper together and see what else God's Word has to say about humble?

Lord, you have heard the desire of the humble: you will prepare their heart, you will cause your ear to hear.

Psalm 10:17 (akjv)

What an amazing verse found in the Psalms! Even the desire of the humble will be heard and the heart of the humble will be prepared which, in the Hebrew is the word כּוּן "kuwn." This means the heart of the humble will be firm, stable, and established! The hearts of so many are unstable and have no foundation, yet God promises to the humble that their heart will be on a firm and secure footing! Wow! What a "benny" to living in humble. A humble heart is a heart that God says he'll make secure, he'll make firm and stable. The word "kuwn" also means to have everything arranged and in order. If more people would humble themselves, then more people would be secure, firm, and established in the things of God rather than wandering in a wilderness of insecurity. Finally, God's ear will literally be "sharp" and "give attention" to those who are praying with a heart of humble. I don't know about you, but I really want

God to pay attention when I pray. I hope you're beginning to see how important humble is in your relationship with God. The humble life begins with a heart that is responsive and tender before God and never filled with pride or arrogance.

For thus says the High and Lofty One Who inhabits eternity, whose name is Holy: "I dwell in the high and holy place, with him who has a contrite and humble spirit, to revive the spirit of the humble, and to revive the heart of the contrite ones (Isaiah 57:15, NKJV).

Do you know that God is the Almighty God, the Alpha and Omega, the First and the Last, the One that is above all, for he is the creator of all? Yet this God who is omnipotent chooses to dwell among people who are humble? In fact, when you live the humble life you'll be living close to God. That's right! God is near the humble. Many of you have probably heard about different times of revival in the history of the church. Could it be that revival came to those who were humble and therefore making room for the revival? This scripture in Isaiah says that God will revive the spirit of those who are making themselves humble and who are contrite before him. Now we must take a few minutes to break this down.

The word in the Hebrew for "dwell" is שכן **shakan**. It means that God chooses to abide and live with those who are humble and "contrite" דכא **dakka'** which is the word for "very much crushed," "broken very small," and literally "dust." God says the kind of people he's going to live with are those who understand how small and low they are and how big and awesome God is. These are the people that

God wants to revive. This is repeated in the Hebrew two times in this scripture that revival belongs to those who make themselves small and humble in relationship to the greatness of God. Now, I'm not talking about making yourself small in the sight of man. There are times in your life that for Christ's sake or kingdom you will humble yourself before a man, but in reality, it will only appear before man that you've made yourself low. It will, in actuality, be before your God. Now, this scripture in Isaiah is, what I believe, Jesus was using as a reference in this teaching on "it is better to fall on the rock then letting the rock fall on you."

The one who falls on this stone will be broken to pieces, and the one on whom it falls will be crushed.
Mathew 21:44 (NET BIBLE)

Again, it's God's desire that we humble ourselves and make our pride break before him rather than let the awesomeness of God fall on us like it did Pharaoh, who refused to let God's people leave the bondages of Egypt. Pride will always cause God to resist us, and eventually no man will be able to stand in the presence of God without being humbled. An example of this is found in Leviticus describing what would happen to the children of Israel if they refused to be humble and obey God's Word.

I will break the pride of your power; I will make your heavens like iron and your earth like bronze. And your strength shall be spent in vain; for your land shall not yield its produce, nor shall the trees of the land yield their fruit. 'Then, if you walk contrary to Me, and are not willing to

obey Me, I will bring on you seven times more plagues, according to your sins.
Leviticus 26:19–21 (NKJV)

Today we think being humble is optional, like having a side of mayo or a pickle on a burger. We don't realize, "No humble no burger!"

Now, I'm writing this to those who will live in the power of humble. I'm not trying to bring us back into an Old Testament or fearful mind-set, but the reality of God's Word is the same regardless concerning the proud and those who will live humble. Let's keep digging! Look what the prophet Samuel spoke to King Saul:

So Samuel said, "When you were little in your own eyes, were you not head of the tribes of Israel? And did not the Lord anoint you king over Israel? 1 Samuel 15:33 (NKJV)

When Saul was young, he was humble and had no trouble making himself low, but now that he's older and the anointed king, he's no longer humble. He wants the recognition and rewards that men can give him. He didn't lead in humility. Instead he used his authority to disobey what God had commanded him to do. In this same passage of scripture, all Saul cared about was that the people honored him as king. He even made the prophet walk with him in a pretense of worship before the Lord. Now because of Saul not humbling himself, when he was confronted with his disobedience and sin, he lost the kingdom, and it was later given to a man by the name of David. Although David wasn't a perfect man, he was a humble man. Now if we were counting sins we would find that it is actually David who is more disobedient than Saul. For years, I have taught in my church, and many of you have heard that "David was a man after God's heart!"

And afterward they asked for a king; so God gave them Saul the son of Kish, a man of the tribe of Benjamin, for forty years. And when He had removed him, He raised up for them David as king, to whom also He gave testimony and said, "I have found David the son of Jesse, a man after My own heart, who will do all My will."
Acts 13:21–22 (NKJV)

Now how could it be that the man after God's own heart was an adulterer, a murderer of many and a disengaged father to his children? I don't know if David qualifies as the man that I want to tell people to follow when it comes to a heart after God based on all human failures. So here we have two men who both have a track record of disobeying God, yet one of them God receives and is exalted as one of Israel's greatest kings and one of them God rejects. Why? Likewise, you who are less experienced, submit to leaders. Further, all of you should clothe yourselves in humility toward one another, because God opposes the arrogant, but to the humble, he gives grace. Therefore, humble yourselves under the mighty hand of God so that at the right time he may lift you up (1 Peter 5:5–6, CJB).

Now let's look at the difference between how David and Saul respond when confronted by the prophet about each of their own personal disobedience. Look at the story of Saul first:

Then the Lord said to Samuel, "I am sorry that I ever made Saul king, for he has not been loyal to me and has refused to obey my command." Samuel was so deeply moved when he heard this that he cried out to the Lord all night. Early the next morning Samuel went to find Saul. Someone told him, "Saul went to the town of Carmel to set up a monument to himself; then he went on to Gilgal."When Samuel finally found him, Saul greeted him cheerfully. "May the Lord bless you," he said. "I have carried out the Lord's command!" "Then what is all the bleating of sheep and goats and the lowing of cattle I hear?" Samuel demanded. "It's true that the army spared the best of the sheep, goats, and cattle," Saul admitted. "But they are going to sacrifice them to the Lord your God. We have destroyed every- thing else. Then Samuel said to Saul, "Stop! Listen to what the Lord told me last night!" "What did he tell you?" Saul asked. And Samuel told him, "Although you may think little of yourself, are you not the leader of the tribes of Israel? The Lord has anointed you king of Israel. And the Lord sent you on a mission and told you, 'Go and completely destroy the sinners, the Amalekites, until they are all dead.' Why haven't you obeyed the Lord? Why did you rush for the plunder and do what was evil in the Lord's sight?" "But I did obey the Lord," Saul insisted. "I carried out the mission he gave me. I brought back King Agag, but I destroyed everyone else. Then my troops brought in the best of the sheep, goats, cattle, and plunder to sacrifice to the Lord your God in Gilgal." But Samuel replied, "What is more pleasing to the Lord: your burnt offerings and sacrifices or your obedience to his voice? Listen! Obedience is better than sacrifice, and submission is better than offering the fat of

rams. Rebellion is as sinful as witchcraft, and stubbornness as bad as worshiping idols. So because you have rejected the command of the Lord, he has rejected you as king."
1 Samuel 15:10–23 (NLT)

We see that Saul is building a monument for himself in the town of Carmel where Samuel as the prophet destroyed 850 false prophets given to Baal and Ashtoreth. Then when Samuel the prophet confronts him with not following the Lord's command, he doesn't repent but denies the disobedience and then persists that his disobedience was only for a good reason, to take the best and sacrifice it to God. I once heard Cindy Trimm quote that *"An excuse is nothing more than a lie wrapped up in the skin of a reason."*

Saul made excuses for his sin and lost everything he had gotten when he forgot the humbleness of small beginnings. In fact, as we read the story of David, we find that he also had small beginnings keeping his father's sheep in the fields, and when the prophet Samuel asked for all of Jesse's sons to come to the feast, David's own father didn't even invite him or consider him a possibility of a future leader or king. So as a young boy, David would recognize the greatness of God in his life and never felt the need to lift himself up or make something happen in his own strength. David lived the humble life and watched how God would take him as a shepherd boy and places him in the king's palace, makes him the king's son-in-law and the captain of the armies of Judah.

When after many years of running and hiding in the

wilderness from a crazy and narcissistic King Saul, David knows one day he will be the king, for he had been anointed with oil by the prophet as a youth. It takes many years and a powerful story of redemption as David finally takes the throne, but what kind of king will he be? Will David follow in Saul's domineering and controlling footsteps, or will David be a different kind of king? In life and in the Bible, it's not how we begin that defines our lives but how we end. Many people, like David and Saul, started out good and with the best of intentions. I don't know of any relationship or marriage that ended because the love was strong in the beginning. It ended because the love didn't keep strong and the end was bitter instead of better. In the case of Saul and David we know Saul had a bitter end and was defeated and left for dead with his son and future posterity in jeopardy. Yet David, who started out good, in the middle gets in trouble when a beautiful and married woman named Bathsheba distracts him. David does more than commit himself to be a voyeur. He allows his lust to drive him to commit adultery with Bathsheba and later has her husband, Uriah, killed along with many others in a cover-up murder battle all devised by the heart of David. Oh, by the way, this is the same man God says is "after my heart!" Are you thinking what I'm thinking right now? David, in the middle of his reign as king, is using his power for himself! He's using his kingly authority to commit adultery and murder, and he almost sounds like some of the leaders of the nations we would say today are evil and full of the devil! Now look at what happens when the prophet Nathan confronts David.

So the Lord sent Nathan to David. When Nathan arrived he said, "There were two men in the same city, one rich, one poor. The rich man had a lot of sheep and cattle, but the poor man had nothing—just one small ewe lamb that he had bought. He raised that lamb, and it grew up with him and his children. It would eat from his food and drink from his cup—even sleep in his arms! It was like a daughter to him. "Now a traveler came to visit the rich man, but he wasn't willing to take anything from his own flock or herd to prepare for the guest who had arrived. Instead, he took the poor man's ewe lamb and prepared it for the visitor. David got very angry at the man, and he said to Nathan, "As surely as the Lord lives, the one who did this is demonic! He must restore the ewe lamb seven times over because he did this and because he had no compassion." "You are that man!" Nathan told David. "This is what the Lord God of Israel says: I anointed you king over Israel and delivered you from Saul's power. I gave your master's house to you, and gave his wives into your embrace. I gave you the house of Israel and Judah. If that was too little, I would have given even more. Why have you despised the Lord's word by doing what is evil in his eyes? You have struck down Uriah the Hittite with the sword and taken his wife as your own. You used the Ammonites to kill him. Because of that, because you despised me and took the wife of Uriah the Hittite as your own, the sword will never leave your own house. "This is what the Lord says: I am making trouble come against you from inside your own family. Before your very eyes I will take your wives away and give them to your friend, and he will have sex with your wives in broad daylight. You did what you did secretly, but I will do what I am doing before all Israel in the light of day." "I've sinned against the Lord!" David said to Nathan. "The Lord has removed your sin," Nathan replied to David. "You won't die. 2 Samuel 12:1–13 (CEB)

The prophet Nathan confronted David and David, unlike Saul, didn't make any excuses for his sins. He immediately took ownership of what he had done and with a repentant heart confessed his sin against the Lord. In the book of Psalms we really see David's heart of remorsefulness and repentance before His God.

Have mercy upon me, O God, according to Your lovingkindness; according to the multitude of Your tender mercies, blot out my transgressions. Wash me thoroughly from my iniquity, and cleanse me from my sin. Create in me a clean heart, O God, and renew a steadfast spirit within me. Do not cast me away from Your presence, And do not take Your Holy Spirit from me. Restore to me the joy of Your salvation, and uphold me by Your generous Spirit. Then I will teach transgressors Your ways, And sinners shall be converted to You. Deliver me from the guilt of bloodshed, O God, The God of my salvation, and my tongue shall sing aloud of Your righteousness. O Lord, open my lips, and my mouth shall show forth Your praise. For You do not desire sacrifice, or else I would give it; You do not delight in burnt offering. The sacrifices of God are a broken spirit, a broken and a contrite heart—These, O God, You will not despise. Psalm 51:1–2, 10–17 (NKJV)

Now do you see the difference between the heart of Saul and the heart of David? Do you see what I've been alluding to about what it was about David's heart that God loved and couldn't resist? I'm going to be real plain and tell you what the difference was between Saul and David. Saul was proud and David was humble! They both started out the same, but David, when he found himself in the error of his ways, went back to the small beginnings of humble and quickly repented, unlike Saul who continued to make excuses. I believe the heart of David is the humble heart and the humble life God wants for us today. Remember, it's not how we start out but how we finish that really matters. There are times in our lives when we can lose our way and get distracted, but that doesn't mean it's over for us. In your journey isn't the promise of perfection but of redemption! Perfection will come when Jesus comes back, but until then, our path is one that gets brighter each day as we walk with God in the power of humble. The more we live in humble, the more we give God permission to work because we are in a constant state and place of receiving rather than repelling. I believe the heart that makes itself low in true humility before God is the one who will see real, genuine revival. Again, this is truly the upside of down!

In the days of the Azusa street revival, the leader was a black man named William Seymour. This was in the early part of the twentieth century, and there was much prejudice in this nation. In California, God began to move in a little house on Bonnie Brae Street. People began to come from all over the world so they moved to a rundown, barn-type building on 916 Azusa Street. It was there that this one-eyed black man would get down on his knees and put his head under a large box or crate of some kind during services that would last throughout the night. Can you imagine today going to a church where the main preacher would do such a thing? People would be saying, "Where is the pastor?" Someone might say, "He is the one with his head under the crate and we don't know when he'll come out from under it." Yet this is exactly what happened on Azusa Street, and if you don't know the story, that small, humble place and that man that made himself low was used by God to spread revival and birth an awakening that has transformed the church around the globe. There are stories of miracles as William Seymour stayed humble under a crate and made a place for God to work. In fact, I have heard that the revival in Azusa actually stopped because other leaders convinced Seymour that it wasn't acceptable behavior for him as the leader to keep his head under a crate! I know it sounds crazy, but maybe we need some leaders today who would be as humble as Seymour. If revival comes to the humble like Isaiah 57 says, we better get back to living a humble life. Maybe we will see something even better than what happened in Azusa. What if you would start living a humble life? What would happen if the people in your church would start doing the same thing? What would happen if we would be quick like David to repent instead of making excuses like Saul? Perhaps God is anticipating for the 2 Chronicles 7:14 generation: a people who humble them- selves and not cry out for the humility of our political and spiritual leaders when we ourselves are not first falling on the rock and letting that rock, which is Christ, direct the steps of our lives with humility. Those who choose to live the humble life will attract the grace that pride repels. Living the humble Upside of down life is living with this prophetic intention:

So rend your heart, and not your garments; Return to the Lord your God, for He is gracious and merciful, slow to anger, and of great kindness; and He relents from doing harm. Joel 2:13 (NKJV)

In your journey isn't the promise of perfection but of redemption!

CHAPTER FIVE:

A Long and Slow Death!

AS FAR AS prophets are concerned in the Old Testament there is perhaps no one greater than Moses, who is known in Numbers as the most humble man upon the face of the whole earth. I want to take you into the life of Moses and want you to hear and see his story, and of course the prophetic destiny that was given to him before he was in his mother's womb. In fact, that's where I want to start. You see, Moses was born in a very turbulent time in the nation of Israel's history. God had brought Israel to live in Egypt, specifically the town of Goshen through a powerful story of redemption as Joseph, the favorite son of Israel, is left for dead and sold into slavery in Egypt. Now Joseph himself was known as a dreamer because of the dreams he had and told his family. The brothers looked at the telling of these dreams as arrogance, and these dreams confirmed and fueled the fire of jealousy over the favoritism of Israel. Joseph's father had also made him a special coat of many colors that identified him all the more as the favorite son, as he was also the son of the wife Rachel, whom

Jacob loved more than their mother Leah. Family rivalry isn't something new, but despite the evil that was done to Joseph, God used it to send Joseph to Egypt and eventually to be the second most powerful man in Egypt. Because of a worldwide famine, Jacob sent his sons to buy food in Egypt. It was there that Joseph eventually revealed himself and his love for his brothers in spite of the evil that was done to him. Joseph sent wagons home with the brothers to fetch his Father and all his relatives to live in Goshen where Joseph would make sure they would be well taken care of. The Bible says this:

A new king came to power in Egypt who didn't know Joseph. He spoke to his people in alarm, "There are way too many of these Israelites for us to handle. We've got to do something: Let's devise a plan to contain them, lest if there's a war they should join our enemies, or just walk off and leave us." So they organized them into work- gangs and put them to hard labor under gang-foremen. They built the storage cities Pithom and Rameses for Pharaoh. But the harder the Egyptians worked them the more children the Israelites had—children everywhere! The Egyptians got so they couldn't stand the Israelites and treated them worse than ever, crushing them with slave labor. They made them miserable with hard labor—making bricks and mortar and back breaking work in the fields. They piled on the work, crushing them under the cruel workload. The king of Egypt had a talk with the two Hebrew midwives; one was named Shiphrah and the other Puah. He said, "When you deliver the Hebrew women, look at the sex of the baby. If it's a boy, kill him; if it's a girl, let her live." But the midwives had far too much respect for God and didn't do what the king of Egypt ordered; they let the boy babies live. The king of Egypt called in the midwives. "Why didn't you obey my orders? You've let those babies live!" The midwives answered Pharaoh, "The Hebrew women aren't like the Egyptian women; they're vigorous. Before the midwife can get there, they've already had the baby." God was pleased with the midwives. The people continued to increase in number—a very strong people. And because the midwives honored God, God gave them families of their own. So Pharaoh issued a general order to all his people: "Every boy that is born, drown him in the Nile. But let the girls live." Exodus 1:8–21 (THE MESSAGE)

The season of favor that brought Israel (Jacob) and his family into Egypt had ended. Now the Egyptians out of fear began to hate the swift multiplication of the Jewish people and did whatever they could to break and bind them. What Egypt and probably Israel had forgotten was that their very journey was given to another dreamer named Abraham who, in horror, saw his future people in slavery in Egypt for 430 years, but then would come out with a great deliverance. So the stage is set and Moses is one of the Hebrew babies pre-served alive by having him float in the Nile directed by his sister, Miriam, to Pharaoh's daughter who, when she sees the little boy floating in the ark, has compassion on him, perhaps because of not having her own child and desires to have one of the Hebrew maids take care of him until he is weaned. Now favor was upon Miriam who brought Moses back to his mother who is now getting paid to take care of her own son. As time passes, Moses is raised in the house of Pharaoh and according to the Bible:

Moses was taught all the wisdom of the Egyptians, and he was powerful in both speech and action.

Acts 7:22 NIV

It was this Moses who never forgot who he was and
apparently had the knowledge that God had put him in the
palace as a son to one day rescue his people from the
tyranny, bondage and cruelty of Egypt. Let's look at the
martyr Stephen's recount of the story of Moses:

"One day when Moses was forty years old, he decided to
visit his relatives, the people of Israel. He saw an Egyptian
mistreating an Israelite. So Moses came to the man's
defense and avenged him, killing the Egyptian. Moses
assumed his fellow Israelites would realize that God had
sent him to rescue them, but they didn't. "The next day he
visited them again and saw two men of Israel fighting. He
tried to be a peacemaker. 'Men,' he said, 'you are brothers.
Why are you fighting each other?' "But the man in the
wrong pushed Moses aside. 'Who made you a ruler and
judge over us?' he asked. 'Are you going to kill me as you
killed that Egyptian yesterday? 'When Moses heard that, he
fled the country and lived as a foreigner in the land of
Midian. There his two sons were born. "Forty years later, in
the desert near Mount Sinai, an angel appeared to Moses in
the flame of a burning bush. When Moses saw it, he was
amazed at the sight. As he went to take a closer look, the
voice of the Lord called out to him, 'I am the God of your
ancestors—the God of Abraham, Isaac, and Jacob.' Moses
shook with terror and did not dare to look. "Then the Lord
said to him, 'Take off your sandals, for you are standing on
holy ground. I have certainly seen the oppression of my
people in Egypt. I have heard their groans and have come
down to rescue them. Now go, for I am sending you back to
Egypt.' "So God sent back the same man his people had

previously rejected when they demanded, 'Who made you a ruler and judge over us?' Through the angel who appeared to him in the burning bush, God sent Moses to be their ruler and savior. And by means of many wonders and miraculous signs, he led them out of Egypt, through the Red Sea, and through the wilderness for forty years.
Acts 7:22–25 (NLT)

Now Moses, at forty years old, sees the injustice done to his people takes matters into his own hands and kills an Egyptian who is beating one of his blood brothers. Moses assumes this is the time and Israel will recognize him as their deliverer. But Moses didn't get the reaction he thought. Instead, he got rejection and a humiliating statement and railing accusation of "who made you our ruler and a judge over us?" Think how Moses must have felt now that he steps up and begins to do what he thinks is his destiny and life mission but gets only suspicion and rejection from his people. Now soon after this incident is made known to Pharaoh, who now seeks to kill Moses, in fear and confusion Moses flees into the wilderness where he remains on the backside of the desert for the next forty years of his life. We find an interesting verse in Acts that talks about Moses's mind-set.

And he supposed that his brethren understood that God was granting them deliverance through him, but they did not understand. Acts 7:25 (NASB)

We can gather from this scripture that Moses, at 40 years old, believed with all his heart that God had sent him to deliver his people even though they didn't receive him. According to the dream that Abraham had it would be a

430-year span of time that the children of Israel would spend in Egypt. Now, it had only been 390 years, and it would take another 40 years for Moses and his people to go through a humbling process so they could freely receive the deliverance God would bring to the people he loved. So it was during the next 40 years of Moses's life that I would like to call "the long and slow death of pride." Pride doesn't die quickly and as long as Moses relied on his own ability, pedigree and power he wouldn't see the interconnected destinies of the children of Israel and their anointed deliverer intersect in the way God desired. So now two things are happening simultaneously during these forty years. First, we find the dream and desire for delivering God's people from Egypt drying up and dying. Any hope would be gone as Moses's influence, strength, and age are all factors working against him as he goes through a long and slow dying process in the wilderness. Now put yourself in the place of Moses. His life begins in a prophetic and powerful way as he lives as a son to Pharaoh in the glory and splendor of Egypt, who is so far ahead of all the cultures of their day. But now at 80 years old, the possibility or dream of deliverance and destiny is now dead. Do you know what else died in Moses? It was pride! Moses had no expectation of his own power or abilities; the only hope for Moses would be a miracle working God. What Moses probably didn't realize is that Abraham foresaw the day that a deliverer would rise up and do the impossible. You might be thinking, "How do you know Moses pride died in the wilderness?"

Moses was a very humble man, more humble than anyone else on earth.
Numbers 12:3 (GWT)

According to this scripture, there wasn't anyone on the entire earth that was as humble as Moses. In fact, the Hebrew in this scripture is even more profound. The word for "very" in the Hebrew is the word מאד (m@`od), and it means "exceedingly, abundantly and greatly."5

So what was Moses exceedingly, abundantly, and greatly in? He was exceedingly, abundantly and greatly humble! In fact, the Hebrew says Moses was ענו transliterated as "anav," then "anav" again! So if this scripture were written to coincide with the actual Hebrew understanding it would read, "The man Moses was exceedingly, abundantly and greatly humble! Humble! And by the way, he's the most humble man on the face of the earth!" Are you getting this?

Moses isn't just a humble man; he exceeds and is great in the humble category. This man is so humble that not a person on the earth is as humble as him.

So now after forty years in the wilderness, something definitely has happened to Moses. Also, I believe while the pride of Moses was dying, the children of Israel, during those last forty years of cruelty and bondage, began to cry out for deliverance like never before. They too had no hope in themselves for destiny and deliverance and they, too, were now a humble people ready for God to show his grace. Again, God always "resists the proud but gives grace to the humble" (James 4:6, NKJV). Now the long, slow death of pride has given way to amazing grace!

After forty years in the wilderness, Moses had a supernatural encounter with God when He turned aside to see a burning bush that was not consumed. The fact that

Moses turned aside to see the bush and hear God's voice confirms the scripture that "the humble shall hear" (Psalm 34:2, NKJV).

Now Moses was pasturing the flock of Jethro his father- in-law, the priest of Midian; and he led the flock to the west side of the wilderness and came to Horeb, the mountain of God. The angel of the Lord appeared to him in a blazing fire from the midst of [a bush; and he looked, and behold, the bush was burning with fire, yet the bush was not consumed. So Moses said, "I must turn aside now and see this marvelous sight, why the bush is not burned up." When the Lord saw that he turned aside to look, God called to him from the midst of the bush and said, "Moses, Moses!" And he said, "Here I am." Then He said, "Do not come near here; remove your sandals from your feet, for the place on which you are standing is holy ground."

He said also, "I am the God of your father, the God of Abraham, the God of Isaac, and the God of Jacob." Then Moses hid his face, for he was afraid to look at God. The Lord said, "I have surely seen the affliction of My people who are in Egypt, and have given heed to their cry because of their taskmasters, for I am aware of their sufferings. So I have come down to deliver them from the power of the Egyptians, and to bring them up from that land to a good and spacious land, to a land flowing with milk and honey, to the place of the Canaanite and the Hittite and the Amorite and the Perizzite and the Hivite and the Jebusite. Now, behold, the cry of the sons of Israel has come to Me; furthermore, I have seen the oppression with which the Egyptians are oppressing them. Therefore, come now, and I will send you to Pharaoh, so that you may bring My people, the sons of Israel, out of Egypt." But Moses said to God, "Who am I, that I should go to Pharaoh, and that I should bring the sons of Israel out of Egypt?" And He said, "Certainly I will be with you, and this shall be the sign to you that it is I who have sent you: when you have brought the people out of Egypt, you shall worship God at this mountain." Exodus 3:1–12 (NASB)

So after forty years, the long, slow death of pride has truly died in Moses. The encounter with the God of the burning bush is the first time the scripture records that Moses had ever heard the voice of God during his now eighty years of living. Before this day of hearing God's voice, we know according to Stephen's words in the book of Acts that Moses had supposed that he was to be received as a deliverer. Nowhere do we find in the Bible of Moses having received a call or mandate from God to do this until his encounter with God in the desert. I believe many times the desert places or wilderness times in our lives can serve as a backdrop for the things to dry up and die that need to die, but we won't let go of unless we're in a desert.

The desert can also serve as a place for us to lose all other distractions and hear what God wants us to hear.

It is amazing what can happen when, like Moses, we don't rely on our own strength anymore. Moses feels completely inadequate in every way to be the deliverer of Israel from Egypt and that's exactly how God wants it. When Moses's pride fully dies, it's at the end of the second generation of his life.

The first forty years, he spends in Egypt as a son of Pharaoh. I believe he was learning pride from the best of best! Then Moses flees and spends the next forty years of his life in the wilderness as the long slow death of pride is completed. Finally, to begin the next season of Moses's life, a new Moses is resurrected as he begins his next forty years with an ear to hear and eyes to see what God wants to do through a truly humble man. Since in the Bible a generation is considered to be forty years, we can assume his life was divided into three distinct divisions. It's in the last forty years of Moses life that he lives in true humble greatness. The more humble a man Moses became, the more God had the opportunity to show His power and grace in his life. Now I hope you and I don't have to wait until we're eighty years old to go through the long, slow death of pride and live in the greatness of humble. In fact, I don't believe we have to. I believe the scriptures and stories of the Bible were written so we don't have to learn the hard way. We can learn by revelation of the Word and not just experience. Truthfully, if I can learn from someone else's experiences of what not to do or what I should do, I'll do it. Let's look at how God feels about this humble, humble man.

Miriam and Aaron began to talk against Moses because of his Cushite wife, for he had married a Cushite. "Has the Lord spoken only through Moses?" they asked. "Hasn't he also spoken through us?" And the Lord heard this. (Now Moses was a very humble man, more humble than anyone else on the face of the earth.) At once the Lord said to Moses, Aaron and Miriam, "Come out to the tent of meeting, all three of you." So the three of them went out. Then the Lord came down in a pillar of cloud; he stood at the entrance to the tent and summoned Aaron and Miriam. When the two of them stepped forward, he said, "Listen to my words: "When there is a prophet among you, I, the Lord, reveal myself to them in visions, I speak to them in dreams. But this is not true of my servant Moses; he is faithful in all my house. With him I speak face to face, clearly and not in riddles; he sees the form of the Lord. Why then were you not afraid to speak against my servant Moses? The anger of the Lord burned against them, and he left them. Numbers 12:1–9 (NIV)

We find that, even though Moses has no more pride left in him and is known by God as the most humble man on the earth, his brother and sister don't agree with Moses's decision when it came to marrying an Ethiopian woman. Now the decision Moses made to marry this woman was personal and didn't affect his ability to lead God's people, and yet Miriam and Aaron began to meddle and gossip about their brother, Moses. Humble leaders who choose to boast in the Lord and not in themselves find no need to defend or explain every decision they make. Also, because humble people aren't always asserting their authority, some may think it is acceptable behavior to speak negatively and unjustly against the humble person. Because proud people will always find fault or are jealous, they think of humble as weak and think they can run all over the people walking and living the Upside of Down humble life. So as Miriam and Aaron speak against Moses, it's not without consequence or defense from God himself. God speaks loud and clear about his unique and special relation- ship with Moses. God says that, "Moses isn't just a prophet; he is one I speak face to face with as a friend who is faithful over everyone else I know" (Exodus 33:11, NKJV). God not only

99

defends Moses and his relationship with him, but a curse of leprosy is released upon Miriam because of their sin. If you begin to see this happen to you as you begin to walk in humble, be like Moses and don't defend yourself. Let God defend you like he did Moses and believe me, as you keep yourself humble before God, you'll be making room for God's grace, and grace can defend and take care of you like nobody can.

Did you know that "Humble technology is not transferable?

Even after Moses was humbled for forty years, it took another forty years to teach the children of Israel, whom Moses led, to be humble as well? There's a truth here that I want you to see. "Humble technology is not transfcrable!" Every one of us has to have a personal encounter and revelation of humble and learn how to live the humble life.

Remember how the Lord your God led you through the wilderness for these forty years, humbling you and testing you to prove your character, and to find out whether or not you would obey his commands. Yes, he humbled you by letting you go hungry and then feeding you with manna, a food previously unknown to you and your ancestors. He did it to teach you that people do not live by bread alone; rather, we live by every word that comes from the mouth of the Lord. For all these forty years your clothes didn't wear out, and your feet didn't blister or swell.
Deuteronomy 8:2–4 (NLT)

Now the long slow death of pride is not only found in the story of Moses. It's also found in the life of others in the Bible such as Joseph. I think it would be good for you to understand that "knowledge puffs up" (1 Corinthians 8:1, NKJV). This means that the more knowledge a person has, the more they tend to have an inflated opinion and pride because of that knowledge. Now the scary thing about knowledge is that it doesn't matter where the knowledge comes from, it will always tend to cause us to have to deal with pride because of that knowledge. So whenever you know something that someone else doesn't or hasn't received yet, it might lead to some pride because of that knowledge. The knowledge could come in the form of a dream a vision or even a revelation from God, and yet that good thing, when not received with humility, will cause some issues. So for instance, when Joseph has dreams of his family bowing before him, this good thing caused pride in him. The dreams were from God, and the dreams would eventually come to pass, yet those dreams were not being received in humility, and in his immaturity, Joseph told his dreams to those who weren't ready to receive them. This caused his brothers to hate him.

Joseph's brothers saw that their father loved him more than any of them. They hated Joseph and couldn't speak to him on friendly terms. Joseph had a dream and when he told his brothers, they hated him even more (Genesis 37:4, 5 GW).

So now Joseph and his pride will go through a dying process, and again, it will be a long, slow death because pride doesn't ever want to die. Now Joseph was only seventeen when he went to Egypt as a slave, and yet everywhere Joseph went, he was blessed and a blessing to those around him. When he is sold into Potiphar's house look at what happens.

Joseph had been taken to Egypt. Potiphar, one of Pharaoh's Egyptian officials and captain of the guard, bought him from the Ishmaelites who had taken him there. The Lord was with Joseph, so he became a successful man. He worked in the house of his Egyptian master. Joseph's master saw that the Lord was with him and that the Lord made everything he did successful. Potiphar liked Joseph so much that he made him his trusted servant. He put him in charge of his household and everything he owned. From that time on the Lord blessed the Egyptian's household because of Joseph. Therefore, the Lord's blessing was on everything Potiphar owned in his house and in his fields. So he left all that he owned in Joseph's care. He wasn't concerned about anything except the food he ate.
Genesis 39:1–6 (GW)

Now during this time, Joseph is a happy Jew serving in the house of Potiphar, but Potiphar's wife tries to seduce Joseph, and when he refuses to yield to her advances, her scorn causes her to accuse Joseph unjustly of rape. Joseph is thrown in prison where he again finds favor and ends up running the prison. While in the prison, Joseph interprets the dream of the butler and the baker of the king and asks the butler to please remember him before the king as Joseph explained all the injustices he had been through. Now at that time, Joseph was defending himself and doing everything in his own power to get out of the prison. Because pride is slow to die, it seems Joseph will still have to wait another two years before the butler does remember him when

Pharaoh has a dream he doesn't understand and they call for Joseph's help. When Joseph comes out of prison and stands before Pharaoh, I believe he stands as a new Joseph and as a man who has no more pride, for it has been a long, slow death, but now Joseph is free from its hold on him.

Then, Pharaoh sent for Joseph, and immediately he was brought from the prison. After he had shaved and changed his clothes, he came in front of Pharaoh. Pharaoh said to Joseph, "I had a dream, and no one can tell me what it means. I heard that when you are told a dream, you could say what it means." Joseph answered Pharaoh, "I can't, but God can give Pharaoh the answer that he needs."
Genesis 41:14–16 (GW)

The humble principle is: Power is never in my own ability but in God's strength that comes by lowering and humbling myself, intentionally making room for grace.

We can now see Joseph with his pride gone, walking and living in the humble principle. For when Joseph speaks to Pharaoh about interpreting his dream, he tells him flat out, "I can't, but god can!" It had taken a long time, but when pride is gone, you and I will say the same. Joseph, now a humble man, would not rely on his abilities or even his dreams but in God's strength and power alone. It's now that Joseph has made room for grace, and he'll see God's grace in a huge way.

Then Pharaoh said to Joseph, "Because God has let you know all this, there is no one as wise and intelligent as you. You will be in charge of my palace, and all my people will

do what you say. I will be more important than you, only because I'm Pharaoh. "Then Pharaoh said to Joseph, "I now put you in charge of Egypt. "Then Pharaoh took off his signet ring and put it on Joseph's finger. He had Joseph dressed in robes of fine linen and put a gold chain around his neck. He had him ride in the chariot of the second in command. Men ran ahead of him and shouted, "Make way!" Pharaoh put Joseph in charge of Egypt.
Genesis 41: 39–41 (GW)

Can you see what great grace was shown Joseph? When pride goes through that long, slow death it makes way for a new, humble person who has made room for God, and grace to show Himself strong. Maybe I forgot to mention that the upside of down sometimes can and will be a little painful. But he sent a man ahead of them, Joseph, who had been sold as a slave. His feet were kept in chains; and an iron collar was around his neck, until what he had predicted came true. The word of the Lord proved him right.
Psalm 105: 17–19 (GNT)

The revelation and dreams God gives us are for us, for our destiny, and yes, even to leave posterity for our children. Testament believers that we too will have to let pride go through that dying process. Hopefully, it won't be a long process either. I believe we need to be like the Apostle Paul who, when he received so much revelation that caused him to be puffed up, had to learn how to "die daily" (1 Corinthians 15:31, NKJV) so as not to live in pride.
One of the most controversial and misunderstood passages of scriptures is "Paul's thorn." Let's read the story:

Yes, only God knows whether I was in my body or outside my body. But I do know that I was caught up to paradise and heard things so astounding that they can- not be expressed in words, things no human is allowed to tell. That experience is worth boasting about, but I'm not going to do it. I will boast only about my weaknesses. If I wanted to boast, I would be no fool in doing so, because I would be telling the truth. But I won't do it, because I don't want anyone to give me credit beyond what they can see in my life or hear in my message, even though I have received such wonderful revelations from God. So to keep me from becoming proud, I was given a thorn in my flesh, a messenger from Satan to torment me and keep me from becoming proud. Three different times I begged the Lord to take it away. Each time he said, "My grace is all you need. My power works best in weakness." So now I am glad to boast about my weaknesses, so that the power of Christ can work through me. That's why I take pleasure in my weaknesses, and in the insults, hardships, persecutions, and troubles that I suffer for Christ. For when I am weak, then I am strong. 2 Corinthians 12:3–9 (NLT)

Now, since we know that the Apostle Paul by inspiration penned about two-thirds of the New Testament and also gave us the wonderful revelation of grace, it's evident that it would be impossible for one to receive these and not have to deal with the potential of being puffed up with pride. Paul has to keep reminding himself of his own personal weakness and the strength that comes from humbling himself. The only way Paul is able to continue to receive revelations from God is in his own personal weakness. So the greatest revelations will always come from those who can maintain and live in the greatness of humble. I'm not saying this is easy or convenient. The very nature of knowledge and revelation will tend to puff up, and we must never allow what we receive or learn to lift ourselves up but instead lift up God who is giving freely to us, as we remain humble before him. The knowledge that has come from God for many has been used as a source of pride and "I know more than you" or "I'm better than you because of this knowledge." This has divided the church into denominations, fractions, and schisms because we've allowed knowledge to puff up instead of living in the simplicity and power of humble. It's now going to take a long, slow death for many in the church to allow their knowledge and need to be right and better to die so revival can come to the humble. May we learn, like Paul, to die daily so that Christ can live through us daily!

My old self has been crucified with Christ. It is no longer I who live, but Christ lives in me. So I live in this earthly body by trusting in the Son of God, who loved me and gave himself for me. Galatians 2:20 (NLT)

It's now going to take a long, slow death for many in the church to allow their knowledge and need to be right and better to die so revival can come to the humble.

CHAPTER SIX:

A Humble Lower Always Leads to Higher

So IF MOSES was the most humble man in his day, what did that humble do for him or should I say through him? Think about this for a moment please. The person whom God used to lead a nation out of bondage and the man God chose to give the Ten Commandments through was Moses. This was also the same man who received the Pentateuch, also known as Torah, from the mouth of God on Mount Sinai. This was also the same man that was desperate for God's presence.

Then Moses said to the Lord, "See, You say to me, 'Bring up this people.' But You have not let me know whom You will send with me. Yet You have said, 'I know you by name, and you have also found grace in My sight.' Now therefore, I pray, if I have found grace in Your sight, show me now Your way, that I may know You and that I may find grace in Your sight. And consider that this nation is Your people." And He said, "My Presence will go with you, and I will give you rest." Then he said to Him, "If Your

Presence does not go with us, do not bring us up from here. For how then will it be known that Your people and I have found grace in Your sight, except You go with us? So we shall be separate, Your people and I, from all the people who are upon the face of the earth." So the Lord said to Moses, "I will also do this thing that you have spoken; for you have found grace in My sight, and I know you by name." And he said, "Please, show me Your glory." Then He said, "I will make all My goodness pass before you, and I will pro- claim the name of the Lord before you. I will be gracious to whom I will be gracious, and I will have compassion on whom I will have compassion." But He said, "You cannot see My face; for no man shall see Me, and live." And the Lord said, "Here is a place by Me, and you shall stand on the rock. So it shall be, while My glory passes by, that I will put you in the cleft of the rock, and will cover you with My hand while I pass by. Then I will take away My hand, and you shall see My back; but My face shall not be seen. Exodus 33:12–23 (NKJV)

Moses was so humble and dependent on God that he refused to go without God's presence anywhere.

Moses was so humble and dependent on God that he refused to go without God's presence anywhere. Now this Scripture is after Moses has brought the people out of Egypt with the signs and wonders that are still talked about today. Do you know of anyone else that has seen a Red Sea part with walls of water on each side so millions of people could pass through and then, by the way, watch those same walls come down upon Pharaoh's army? Yet this man Moses says that he desires more. In fact, he asks God to show him the glory of God. Because this is Old Testament and before

Jesus manifesting himself in the flesh, God cannot fully show Moses his glory because the glory of God is Jesus.

And the Word became flesh and dwelt among us, and we beheld His glory, the glory as of the only begotten of the Father, full of grace and truth.
John 1:14 (NKJV)

God told Moses to stand in the cleft of the rock, which was a type and shadow of what was to come, as we now who believe are standing in the cleft of the rock that is Christ, the hope of glory. Now because of Moses humility, God grants him a glimpse of what is to come. But let me show you what happens in the future. When Jesus does come in the flesh, God uses the opportunity to answer Moses's prayer to see God's glory.

Now after six days Jesus took Peter, James, and John his brother, led them up on a high mountain by themselves; and He was transfigured before them. His face shone like the sun, and His clothes became as white as the light. And behold, Moses and Elijah appeared to them, talking with Him. Then Peter answered and said to Jesus, "Lord, it is good for us to be here; if You wish, let us make here three tabernacles: one for You, one for Moses, and one for Elijah." While he was still speaking, behold, a bright cloud overshadowed them; and suddenly a voice came out of the cloud, saying, "This is My beloved Son, in whom I am well pleased. Hear Him!" And when the disciples heard it, they fell on their faces and were greatly afraid. But Jesus came and touched them and said, "Arise, and do not be afraid." When they had lifted up their eyes, they saw no one but Jesus only. Now as they came down from the mountain,

Jesus commanded them, saying, "Tell the vision to no one until the Son of Man is risen from the dead."
Matthew 17:1–9 (NKJV)

Today if we want something to be exposed, we commercialize it, advertise it, and over emphasize it.

Do you realize what happened right before the eyes of the three disciples? Jesus manifests himself as the glory of God and who else do we find here? Who was there to see God's glory? It was Moses who had prayed thousands of years earlier and asked God to see his glory. I believe, again this confirms what God will do when we are truly humble before him. God will move heaven, earth, or even translate a person in and out of time to answer their prayer. So Moses got to see the glory of God after all, in all his splendor and majesty.

Now even though Moses was the most humble man of his day, there's another man that will actually be the most humble man who ever lived or walked the earth. The man is of course Jesus, and even in his birth we see his humble beginnings of being laid in a feeding trough and quite probably born in the temporary shelter of a Sukkah. This same Jesus also grew up without much fanfare except when he was two years old; the coming of the wise men with the gold, frankincense, and myrrh. Jesus learned the trade of his father, and there's only one reference to Jesus at twelve years old astounding the teachers in the temple with his knowledge of the scriptures. So Jesus at the age of thirty starts his ministry by spending time in prayer.

Jesus went up on a mountain and called those he wanted, and they came to him. He appointed twelve and called them apostles. He appointed them to be with him, to be sent out to preach. Mark 3:13–14 (CEB)

So Jesus, while he is doing his ministry, never exalts himself, never praises himself, and in fact tells others not to talk about him. Instead, every reference of exaltation of praise is always to be referred back to Jesus's Father, God. This is a very strange way of building something big, isn't it? Today if we want something to be exposed, we commercialize it, advertise it, and over emphasize it, yet look at how different that is from the way Jesus lived.

Think of yourselves the way Christ Jesus thought of himself. He had equal status with God but didn't think so much of himself that he had to cling to the advantages of that status no matter what. Not at all. When the time came, he set aside the privileges of deity and took on the status of a slave, became human! Having become human, he stayed human. It was an incredibly humbling process. He didn't claim special privileges. Instead, he lived a selfless, obedient life and then died a selfless, obedient death—and the worst kind of death at that—a crucifixion. Because of that obedience, God lifted him high and honored him far beyond anyone or anything, ever, so that all created beings in heaven and on earth—even those long ago dead and buried—will bow in worship before this Jesus Christ, and call out in praise that he is the Master of all, to the glorious honor of God the Father.
Philippians 2:5–8 (MSG)

So Jesus, who is equal with God and the One who created everything, doesn't lean or take that in account when he, as a man walked the earth and laid aside his majesty and glory and clothed himself in the skin of a man. Jesus put on human skin, and as the Word became flesh and "*tabernacled*," if you will, among humanity. Jesus never one time sought recognition or power for his own benefit yet was offered the kingdoms of the world by Satan himself.

Jesus took the test for humanity and proved that humility will always triumph over self-provision, self- preservation and self-promotion.

Next, Jesus was taken into the wild by the Spirit for the Test. The Devil was ready to give it. Jesus prepared for the Test by fasting forty days and forty nights. That left Him, of course, in a state of extreme hunger, which the Devil took advantage of in the first test: "Since You are God's Son, speak the word that will turn these stones into loaves of bread." Jesus answered by quoting Deuteronomy: "It takes more than bread to stay alive. It takes a steady stream of words from God's mouth." For the second test the Devil took him to the Holy City. He sat him on top of the Temple and said, "Since You are God's Son, jump. "The Devil goaded Him by quoting Psalm 91: "He has placed you in the care of angels. They will catch you so that you won't so much as stub your toe on a stone." Jesus countered with another citation from Deuteronomy: "Don't you dare test the Lord your God." For the third test, the Devil took Him to the peak of a huge mountain. He gestured expansively, pointing out all the earth's kingdoms, how glorious they all were. Then he said, "They're Yours—lock, stock, and barrel. Just go down on Your knees and worship me, and

they're Yours." Jesus' refusal was curt: "Beat it, Satan!" He backed His rebuke with a third quotation from Deuteronomy: "Worship the Lord your God, and only him. Serve him with absolute single-heartedness." The Test was over. The Devil left. And in his place, angels! Angels came and took care of Jesus' needs.
Matthew 4:1–11 (MSG)

Jesus took the test for humanity and proved that humility will always triumph over self-provision, self-preservation and self-promotion. Of course, just because Jesus passed the test doesn't mean that Satan won't test you with the same thing. There was something different about Jesus than any other man.

So because Jesus made himself lower than anyone, God would make Jesus higher than anyone. Jesus understood the humble principle and lived his life by it. In fact, Jesus didn't only teach this humble principle, but Jesus modeled and demonstrated it over and over again. If anyone lived the upside of down, it was Yeshua Messiah, Jesus Christ.

The humble principle is "Power is never in my own ability but in God's strength that comes by lowering and humbling myself, intentionally making room for grace."

Please read this story:

Just before the Passover Feast, Jesus knew that the time had come to leave this world to go to the Father. Having loved his dear companions, he continued to love them right to the end. It was suppertime. The Devil by now had Judas, son of Simon the Iscariot, firmly in his grip, all set for the betrayal.

Jesus knew that the Father had put him in complete charge of everything that he came from God and was on his way back to God. So he got up from the supper table, set aside his robe, and put on an apron. Then he poured water into a basin and began to wash the feet of the disciples, drying them with his apron. When he got to Simon Peter, Peter said, "Master, you wash my feet?" Jesus answered, "You don't understand now what I'm doing, but it will be clear enough to you later." Peter persisted, "You're not going to wash my feet—ever! "Jesus said, "If I don't wash you, you can't be part of what I'm doing." "Master!" said Peter. "Not only my feet, then. Wash my hands! Wash my head!" Jesus said, "If you've had a bath in the morning, you only need your feet washed now and you're clean from head to toe. My concern, you understand, is holiness, not hygiene. So now you're clean. But not every one of you." (He knew who was betraying him. That's why he said, "Not every one of you.") After he had finished washing their feet, he took his robe, put it back on, and went back to his place at the table. Then he said, "Do you understand what I have done to you? You address me as 'Teacher' and 'Master,' and rightly so. That is what I am. So if I, the Master and Teacher, washed your feet, you must now wash each other's feet. I've laid down a pattern for you. What I've done, you do. I'm only pointing out the obvious. A servant is not ranked above his master; an employee doesn't give orders to the employer. If you understand what I'm telling you, act like it—and live a blessed life.
John 13:1–17 (MSG)

Jesus, before he ate the final Passover meal with the disciples, did something that might have never been done in the history of mentor to mentee relationships. Of course

114

Jesus was no ordinary mentor. Jesus picks up the towel of servant hood, gets a basin of water, and begins to wash each of his disciples' feet. He even washes Judas' feet knowing that Judas is the one that will ultimately give into the temptation of pride and self-provision by taking a mere thirty pieces of silver for the life of Rabbi Jesus. Because Jesus isn't just doing a prophetic act but demonstrating his life message to " *shama,* " to hear, listen, follow, and obey his Father, this washing of the disciples' feet was also something they could never, ever forget. As they watched the Messiah and Lord of the universe get down on his knees to wash their dirty and dusty feet, it spoke volumes to them and would change the way they would look at Jesus and themselves forever. Because Jesus lived a life dependent on the Father and not his own abilities, there was never any lack or need that stayed unmet. So look how Jesus lived in the principle and power of humble before God, his Father.

Then Jesus answered and said to them, "Most assuredly, I say to you, the Son can do nothing of Himself, but what He sees the Father do; for whatever He does, the Son also does in like manner. I can of Myself do nothing. As I hear, I judge; and My judgment is righteous, because I do not seek My own will but the will of the Father who sent Me.
John 5:19, 30 (NKJV)

Do you see the humility in Jesus? Do you see the humble principle operating in Jesus to the max? Do we see Jesus looking to his own abilities, wisdom, or power? Do you see how Jesus lived and modeled the Upside of Down life?

115

Look at some other scriptures about Jesus living as the most humble man even though he had the right to live as the firstborn Son of the Father.

When a person operates in humble, it's for them to simply be a vessel for God's grace to flow!

Jesus left Tyre and went up to Sidon before going back to the Sea of Galilee and the region of the Ten Towns. A deaf man with a speech impediment was brought to him, and the people begged Jesus to lay his hands on the man to heal him. Jesus led him away from the crowd so they could be alone. He put his fingers into the man's ears. Then, spitting on his own fingers, he touched the man's tongue. Looking up to heaven, he sighed and said, "Ephphatha," which means, "Be opened!" Instantly the man could hear perfectly, and his tongue was freed so he could speak plainly! Jesus told the crowd not to tell anyone, but the more he told them not to, the more they spread the news. They were completely amazed and said again and again, "Everything he does is wonderful. He even makes the deaf to hear and gives speech to those who cannot speak."
Mark 7:31–26 (NLT)

Jesus did miracle after miracle, and nine times in the gospels, Jesus tells the people not to tell anyone. Because Jesus lived by the principle of humble, he didn't want to yield to the self-promotion tactics of others. Instead, Jesus would let the fruit of humility speak for itself, which had far greater impact and results than lifting oneself up. I'm thinking an old school thought right now. Wouldn't these people put themselves in jeopardy of losing their miracles because they didn't obey Jesus when he told them not to tell anyone? If the miracles were based on their works or obedience maybe, but in truth, the miracles were done because Jesus, operating in humble, saw his Father healing, restoring, and raising to life those who were dead. When a person operates in humble, it's for them to simply be a vessel for God's grace to flow. Jesus wasn't just a recipient of the grace to the humble but according to the scriptures was full of grace.

And the Word became flesh and dwelt among us, and we beheld His glory, the glory as of the only begotten of the Father, full of grace and truth. And of His fullness we have all received, and grace for grace. For the law was given through Moses, but grace and truth came through Jesus Christ. John 1:14, 16–17 (NKJV)

Because the church hasn't understood grace and Jesus's ability to transform us through grace, we tend to lean back into guilt, condemnation, and legalism when what we need is grace for grace. I like to teach my people that grace is always unearned, underserved, and unmerited, and you can never work or earn it in any way. The moment you earn grace, it ceases to be grace.

Now grace is supernatural favor released to you and me through Jesus Christ.

This grace is for everyone, but not everyone will make room for it or receive it. The humble will always attract the grace while the proud will always repel the grace. The moment we humble ourselves grace shows up in abundance and changes our lives starting with our hearts and then working outwardly as we continue to yield to it. Jesus, as a man full of grace and completely humble in every way, he never put limits on what was available to those who would yield to receive the power, healing, and miracles that only grace could bring. When the scriptures teach that Jesus healed all, it means all!

So he left that area, and many people followed him. He healed all the sick among them.
Matthew 12:15 (NLT)

The reason again that Jesus healed all is that he, operating in humble, saw his Father healing all, and that's exactly what he did. The only time the "all" didn't get healed was when the people didn't make room for the Man full of grace and despised Jesus because of his supposed lack of pedigree and where he was from.

Jesus left that part of the country and returned with his disciples to Nazareth, his hometown. The next Sabbath he began teaching in the synagogue, and many who heard him were amazed. They asked, "Where did he get all this wisdom and the power to perform such miracles?" Then they scoffed, "He's just a carpenter, the son of Mary and the brother of James, Joseph, Judas, and Simon. And his sisters live right here among us." They were deeply offended and refused to believe in him. Then Jesus told them, "A prophet is honored everywhere except in his own hometown and among his relatives and his own family." And because of their unbelief, he couldn't do any miracles among them except to place his hands on a few sick people and heal them. And he was amazed at their unbelief.
Mark 6:1–6 (NLT)

So now, even though Jesus desired to do what he knew his father had sent him to Nazareth to do, Jesus couldn't do it! This is crazy powerful because the scripture doesn't say he wouldn't, but that he couldn't do any miracles. These people had among them the same Man that would go to other cities and had done so many other miracles.

The moment you earn grace, it ceases to be grace.

Jesus also did many other things. If they were all written down, I suppose the whole world could not contain the books that would be written.
John 21:25 (NLT)

Jesus loves all and died for all, but unless he is received and believed in as the Lord, what Jesus did on the cross won't benefit them. Jesus taught from a unique perspective as one who made himself lower so that he could take man higher. The scriptures prophesied about this kind of a Messiah but few recognized him when he came. The only way to receive Jesus is to humble yourself and believe that he is God! The promise of going higher and the upside of down is modeled by Jesus who is God in the flesh, who intentionally made himself lower as the highest and greatest example of humility and the Upside of Down life anyone will ever see. We know that because Yeshua made himself lower than anyone it would be God the father who would in time exalt him higher than anyone.

Rejoice, O people of Zion! Shout in triumph, O people of Jerusalem! Look, your king is coming to you. He is

righteous and victorious, yet he is humble, riding on a don-key—riding on a donkey's colt.
Zechariah 9:9 (NLT)

So Jesus comes humble and isn't well received, but others who lift themselves up will almost always be received.

For I have come to you in my Father's name, and you have rejected me. Yet if others come in their own name, you gladly welcome them. No wonder you can't believe! For you gladly honor each other, but you don't care about the honor that comes from the one who alone is God.
John 5:43–44 (NLT)

This never ceases to amaze me, but it's as true today as then. People love those who boast about themselves and say they are the greatest. Do you remember Muhammad Ali and how he would boast about how he was the greatest of them all? I can still hear his boasting in his poems like this one:

So don't bet against me, I'm a man of my word. He is the greatest! Yes! I am the man this poem's about, I'll be champ of the world, there isn't a doubt. Here I predict Mr. Liston's dismemberment; I'll hit him so hard; he'll won- der where October and November went. When I say two, there's never a third, Standing against me is completely absurd. When Cassius says a mouse can outrun a horse, Don't ask how; put your money where your mouse is! I AM THE GREATEST! Muhammad Ali

To be honest, I really like Muhammad Ali, for he was wildly entertaining and a good boxer, but oh, so proud. Eventually, he lost his heavyweight crown to another fighter. After all "pride does come before a fall" (Proverbs 16:18, NKJV).

The spirit of self-promotion is also seen in our movies, news, and politics where it seems no one is embracing the genuine power and grace that only humble will attract. Jesus sought to teach his disciples these truths about by being humble himself.

Take my yoke upon you. Let me teach you, because I am humble and gentle at heart, and you will find rest for your souls. Matthew 11:29 (NLT)

The way Jesus teaches is in the old school of apprentice-ship. Today we think if we get a degree from a school we are a master, when many times our degrees aren't worth much more than the paper they're written on because they don't have the real life experience of apprenticeship behind it. Now the key to this method of teaching is being yoked together with the teacher, spending enormous amounts of time with them in order for what they know to brush off into you. Jesus lives a life of humble, and because he humbled himself lower than any man, God lifted Jesus up higher than any man. Jesus is exalted to the right hand of God, and now all creation will one day bow before his throne.

If so, then you and all the people of Israel need to know that this man stands healthy before you because of the name of Jesus Christ the Nazarene—whom you crucified but whom God raised from the dead. This Jesus is the stone you builders rejected; he has become the corner- stone! Salvation can be found in no one else. Throughout the whole world, no other name has been given among humans through which we must be saved.

Acts 4:10–12 (CEB)

*Since a humble lower always leads to a greater
and a higher, how low are you willing to go?*

It's this man Jesus, who lived the epitome of the humble life completely dependent on his Father's power and authority, whom God has chosen to now lift as both Lord and Christ.

Humble yourselves before the Lord, and he will lift you up.
James 4:10 (CEB)

It's the one who is humble before God who will always be lifted up to greatness. It's a principle and law of the kingdom of God. When we lift ourselves up, we'll be humbled, but when we humble ourselves, God will lift us up. In the last days, the scripture teaches that the Antichrist will be one who exalts himself above God and will demand worship by sitting in the temple declaring he to be God. This teaching is found in the Bible in the book of 2 Thessalonians chapter two. Satan has always been in the business of self-promotion and self-exaltation and his infamous words are always "I will." This is in direct conflict and contrast with the humble Servant and the One who introduces himself as the Son of man, even though Jesus could have, without reservation, called himself the Son of God. Today we see the spirit of pride as a counterfeit always competing with those who choose humble. The call to greatness is paved and carved out for those who will humble themselves under the powerful hand of God and allow God to exalt in his good time (1 Peter 5:6, YLT).

Jesus, the Lord and Savior, has set the example for us. Jesus first laid down his will, and after, he laid down his life. The will has to be submitted before anything else. Jesus obeyed the prophetic scriptures concerning this.

This is why, on coming into the world, he says, "It has not been your will to have an animal sacrifice and a meal offering; rather, you have prepared for me a body. No, you have not been pleased with burnt offerings and sin offerings. Then I said, 'Look! In the scroll of the book it is written about me. I have come to do your will.'" In saying first, "You neither willed nor were pleased with animal sacrifices, meal offerings, burnt offerings and sin offerings," things which are offered in accordance with the Torah; and then, "Look, I have come to do your will"; he takes away the first system in order to set up the second. It is in connection with this will that we have been separated for God and made holy, once and for all, through the offering of Yeshua the Messiah's body.
Hebrews 10:5–9 (CJB)

Moses prophesied about a prophet that the people would *shama*. "This is that Moses who said to the children of Israel, 'The Lord your God will raise up for you a Prophet like me from your brethren. Him you shall hear'" (Acts 7:37, NKJV).

Moses and Jesus are more connected than you might realize. For example, God gave Moses the Ten Commandments, which God wrote into stone tablets that God himself cut out of the mountain called Sinai. We know that Moses then took these stones, and, before even presenting them to the people, broke them in pieces because of the idolatry going on in the camp, which was condoned by Moses's brother Aaron. Have you ever wondered why God didn't get mad at Moses for breaking those stones?

And Moses turned and went down from the mountain, and the two tablets of the Testimony were in his hand.
The tablets were written on both sides; on the one side and on the other they were written. Now the tablets were the work of God, and the writing was the writing of God engraved on the tablets. So it was, as soon as he came near the camp, that he saw the calf and the dancing. So Moses' anger became hot, and he cast the tablets out of his hands and broke them at the foot of the mountain.
Exodus 32:15, 16, 18 (NKJV)

I have searched far and wide and can't find where God gets angry with Moses for breaking these stones, which were made and engraved by God himself. When you think about it, Moses was the first man to break all Ten Commandments, literally, that is. Have you ever wondered why God wasn't mad at Moses? One day as I was reading this story, I was quickened to look at what was different about when Moses received the commandments for the second time. Do you know what I found out? The second time God didn't carve the tablets from the rock to write on. Instead, he made Moses do it.

At that time the Lord said to me, "Hew for yourself two tablets of stone like the first, and come up to Me on the mountain and make yourself an ark of wood. And I will write on the tablets the words that were on the first tablets, which you broke; and you shall put them in the ark." So I made an ark of acacia wood, hewed two tablets of stone like

the first, and went up the mountain, having the two tablets in my hand. And He wrote on the tablets according to the first writing, the Ten Commandments, which the Lord had spoken to you in the mountain from the midst of the fire in the day of the assembly; and the Lord gave them to me. Then I turned and came down from the mountain, and put the tablets in the ark which I had made; and there they are, just as the Lord commanded me.
Deuteronomy 10:1–5

So God tells Moses to hew tablets from the mountain, just like he had seen God do the first time, and carry them up to the mountain so God will do the writing. Moses was also told to put those tablets immediately in the ark that he had pre- pared for them. I believe the first tablets that Moses broke were to represent the first man, Adam, who was formed out of the dust by God alone, who then breathed into Adam a life that would eventually die because of sin. We know the first tablets were a work of God alone, and the man, Moses, is only a receiver of the law. The second set of tablets is quite different, for it's a work of man and God. Moses, the man, hews out the stone, and God writes on it. The second set of tablets represents the second Adam, which is Christ. This second man was a work of God and man together as the Spirit of God came upon human flesh to produce the Messiah Jesus. So when the law was given the second time, it was put in an ark of wood with a covering called the mercy seat. The tablets that Moses had carved would remain covered with mercy as a type and shadow of what was to come. God has forever tied himself to humanity as the second Adam took upon himself human flesh and "tabernacle" among us. It's this humble Lord who came down from heaven to be near us, to know us and to free us.

125

It's also this humble Lord who invites us to now come up higher before a throne of mercy and grace by the humble blood that he shed. It's also this Messiah that has forever put the law in an ark of grace covered by his atoning blood. It's in the life of the humble man, Jesus that we find the truth that humble will always lead to greatness. If not in this life, then in the life to come, for the humble will always have a special place in the heart of God. Since a humble lower always leads to a greater and a higher, how low are you willing to go?

Arise, O Lord; O God, lift up your hand: forget not the humble. Psalm 10:12 (NKJV)

CHAPTER SEVEN:

Jesus Teaching on Humble

J ESUS, WHEN HE walked the earth, not only lived as the most humble man ever, but also taught the principle of humble to the multitudes and to his beloved disciples. It was the teaching on humble that really would get the religious leaders filled with anger and rage against Jesus, especially because He refused to play their self-righteous games. Jesus also refused to confine his teachings in the framework of the religious system that required spiritual blindness on the parts of their followers. Because the humble principle doesn't rely on one's own power or ability but God's, it's not uncommon for a humble life to cause those who operate in pride to be very uncomfortable in their presence. The pecking order in society will always push those to the forefront who look the most capable and know how to speak to the baser and lower senses and emotions of people. This many times is in direct contrast with those who, like Jesus, don't find their self-worth or acceptance in temporary power or position but rather in the grace that comes from making room for a power and strength greater than their own.

"It's an upside down kingdom." To go up, you must go down, and to go down, means you will eventually go up.

Jesus does extensive teaching at times to the multitudes and at times more intimately to his small group of disciples. As it is today, just because a message is taught or even modeled, it won't necessarily permeate the layers and levels of belief systems that have been formed and forged within many of us since the days when we were very young. As a pastor, I find I get frustrated by not having more people walk in the power of God's Word. Sometimes I feel like I'm wasting my time, perhaps no one is listening to a word I preach. I suppose I'm not the only preacher who feels like, "Hey, God, no one is listening. Why am I preaching this again?" Now I know that faith comes by "hearing and hearing" or "*shama, shama,*" but man, I sure wish the process of change wouldn't be so slow. Jesus had to deal with this more than once. Please listen:

James and John, Zebedee's sons, came to Jesus and said, "Teacher, we want you to do for us whatever we ask." "What do you want me to do for you?" he asked. They said, "Allow one of us to sit on your right and the other on your left when you enter your glory." Jesus replied, "You don't know what you're asking! Can you drink the cup I drink or receive the baptism I receive?" "We can," they answered. Jesus said, "You will drink the cup I drink and receive the baptism I receive, but to sit at my right or left hand isn't mine to give. It belongs to those for whom it has been prepared." Now when the other ten disciples heard about

this, they became angry with James and John. Jesus called them over and said, "You know that the ones who are considered the rulers by the Gentiles show off their authority over them and their high-ranking officials order them around. But that's not the way it will be with you. Whoever wants to be great among you will be your servant. Whoever wants to be first among you will be the slave of all, for the Human One didn't come to be served but rather to serve and to give his life to liberate many people."
Mark 10: 35–45 (CEB)

The pecking order in society will always push those to the forefront who look the most capable and know how to speak to the baser and lower senses and emotions of people.

I know Jesus wasn't surprised at the request of the sons of Zebedee, but can you believe their gall? I'm Jewish and can tell you myself, I can believe it. I know personally that Jewish people will say and ask things that most others would be too embarrassed or ashamed to say. My sweet, naturally born Gentile wife Lisa, (*Now she's a Hebrew Christian!*) had to cover for me countless of times as I put my foot in my mouth with no indignity at all. (So sorry, baby, I'm trying real hard not to be so Jewish in that respect, but will continue to be Jewish or more accurately a Hebrew when it comes to knowing I'm blessed to be a blessing.) So even though Jesus will continue to train and teach his disciples about humility, they don't seem to get it. Remember, it's not wrong to desire the seats at the top; you just have to know that the best way to get higher in God's kingdom is to go lower. Again, this is the reason for the title of this book Upside of Down. I guess it's true when we say,

129

"It's an upside down kingdom." To go up, you must go down, and to go down, means you will eventually go up.

Jesus said to the crowds and to his disciples: The Pharisees and the teachers of the Law are experts in the Law of Moses. So obey everything they teach you, but don't do as they do. After all, they say one thing and do something else. They pile heavy burdens on people's shoulders and won't lift a finger to help. Everything they do is just to show off in front of others. They even make a big show of wearing Scripture verses on their foreheads and arms, and they wear big tassels for everyone to see. They love the best seats at banquets and the front seats in the meeting places. And when they are in the market, they like to have people greet them as their teachers. But none of you should be called a teacher. You have only one teacher, and all of you are like brothers and sisters. Don't call anyone on earth your father. All of you have the same Father in heaven. None of you should be called the leader. The Messiah is your only leader. Whoever is the greatest should be the servant of the others. If you put yourself above others, you will be put down. But if you humble yourself, you will be honored. Matthew 23:1–12 (CEB)

The word for humble in the Greek language is: ταπεινόω— **Tapeinoō** and according to the Strong's concordance this is what it means:

1.   To make low, bring low
2.   To level, reduce to a plain
3.   Metaphor: to bring into a humble condition, reduce to meaner circumstances
4.   To assign a lower rank or place to

5.   To abase
6.   To be ranked below others who are honored or rewarded
7.   To humble or abase myself by humble living
8.   To lower, depress
9.   Of one's soul bring down one's pride
10.   To have a modest opinion of one's self
11.   To behave in an unassuming manner
12.   Devoid of all haughtiness 7

Jesus was giving the crowds a visual picture of contrast. This is a very traditional way a Rabbi would teach during that day. Please remember that Jesus is not only the Son of Man, but he is also the Word of God made flesh.

See, the Word of God is alive! It is at work and is sharper than any double-edged sword—it cuts right through to where soul meets spirit and joints meet marrow, and it is quick to judge the inner reflections and attitudes of the heart. Hebrews 4:12 (CJB)

Jesus as the Word could look into the thoughts and attitudes of the multitudes listening to him speak and know what they were really thinking. Jesus knew the people deep down could see through the hypocrisy of their leadership. Is it any different today as people put up with the hypocritical actions of politicians with their high ideals for others, but are never accountable to the same ethics and standards? The prideful spirit that was at work in the religious leaders of Jesus's day is no different than what the American culture is now apathetic about because we have come to accept that "this is the way it is and will always be." Jesus, knowing the attitudes and hearts of the people, began to describe the behaviors of their religious leaders in a way that affirmed all that the people already knew, but no one would ever have the courage to say. Jesus, being humble with no skeletons in the closet of his own, could speak freely of the hypocrisy, not to condemn, but to bring light to the truth and power of living humble. So Jesus tells the people unequivocally, "Whoever exalts himself will be humbled, and he who humbles himself will be exalted" (Matthew 23:12, NKJV). Jesus was teaching a foreign language to those religious leaders that heard him. If you read the entire twenty-third chapter of Matthew, you will see Jesus berating the Scribes and Pharisees. Jesus was trying to teach a principle to the people that shouldn't have been foreign to them. It wasn't something really new, just not lived or taught anymore.

For you deliver humble people, but haughty eyes you humiliate. Psalm 18:27 (LEB)

The Lord lifts up the humble; he casts the wicked to the ground. Psalm 147:6 (ESV)

Better to be of a humble spirit with the lowly, Than to divide the spoil with the proud. Proverbs 16:19 (NKJV)

Disperse the rage of your wrath; Look on everyone who is proud, and humble him. Job 40:11 (NKJV)

A man's pride will bring him low, but a humble spirit will obtain honor. Proverbs 29:23 (NASB)

This is what the Sovereign Lord says: "Take off your jeweled crown, for the old order changes. Now the lowly will be exalted, and the mighty will be brought down."

Ezekiel 21:26 (NLT)

Jesus was teaching the same thing that had been written in the scriptures over and over again. Even David, one of the greatest kings of Israel, talked and demonstrated a life of humble.

Now as the ark of the Lord came into the City of David, Michal, Saul's daughter, looked through a window and saw King David leaping and whirling before the Lord; and she despised him in her heart. So they brought the ark of the Lord, and set it in its place in the midst of the tabernacle that David had erected for it. Then David offered burnt offerings and peace offerings before the Lord. And when David had finished offering burnt offerings and peace offerings, he blessed the people in the name of the Lord of hosts. Then he distributed among all the people, among the whole multitude of Israel, both the women and the men, to everyone a loaf of bread, a piece of meat, and a cake of raisins. So all the people departed, everyone to his house. Then David returned to bless his household. And Michal the daughter of Saul came out to meet David, and said, "How glorious was the king of Israel today, uncovering himself today in the eyes of the maids of his servants, as one of the base fellows shamelessly uncovers himself! "So David said to Michal, "It was before the Lord, who chose me instead of your father and all his house, to appoint me ruler over the people of the Lord, over Israel. Therefore I will play music before the Lord. And I will be even more undignified than this, and will be humble in my own sight.

But as for the maidservants of whom you have spoken, by them I will be held in honor." Therefore Michal the daughter of Saul had no children to the day of her death. 2 Samuel 6:16–23 (NKJV)

Jesus's teaching on humble was very profound and more than once did he talk about what happens when you lift your- self up and when you humble yourself what will transpire as well.

When Jesus noticed that all who had come to the dinner were trying to sit in the seats of honor near the head of the table, he gave them this advice: "When you are invited to a wedding feast, don't sit in the seat of honor. What if someone who is more distinguished than you has also been invited? The host will come and say, 'Give this person your seat.' Then you will be embarrassed, and you will have to take whatever seat is left at the foot of the table! "Instead, take the lowest place at the foot of the table. Then when your host sees you, he will come and say, 'Friend, we have a better place for you!' Then you will be honored in front of all the other guests. For those who exalt themselves will be humbled, and those who humble themselves will be exalted." Luke 14:7–11 (NLT)

Jesus desires to teach his followers about the force of humble in their lives. So he tells a parable about something the people could relate to. Again Jesus nudges at the heart of all people who want to be recognized, received with honor, and rewarded. These things aren't evil, negative, or immoral but simply how we're all wired. Jesus then communicates to the people that there is no need for them to go after these things in any way. Jesus is telling the people not to make exalting or prominence happen for yourself or in your own power, exerting your talents, proficiencies, or position to a place of recognition. I also as a pastor have told my leaders that, "In this Church, you never have to lift yourself up in any way. You don't have to show off your personality, your gifting's or your abilities." I also tell them "Not to look for a title to give you recognition. If you are called to do something, just begin to function in that call." I tell them, "The title doesn't make you anything. It's the function that will display your call to all, and no one will be able to deny what God desires to do in and through your life.

I'm also a part of a network called Kingdom Global Ministries led by Larry Titus. Any time we have meetings and events no one is recognized or called with a title in front of their name. We are all brothers and sons of God and have no need to lift ourselves up to prominence, for that's what God has promised to do when we humble ourselves. I want you who are reading this book to realize you never need to exalt or promote yourself to receive the desires of your heart. At the right time, God will lift you up and present you into prominence and honor, but if you do make something happen for yourself, just remember it'll be you who has to maintain and sustain that position. If God does it, he'll be the one who sustains and maintains by his power and not yours, which I believe is a lot better. The blessing of humility will come to anyone who lives the teaching of Jesus about humble. Let's look at some more of Jesus's teaching on humble.

Also He spoke this parable to some who trusted in themselves that they were righteous, and despised others: "Two

135

men went up to the temple to pray, one a Pharisee and the other a tax collector. The Pharisee stood and prayed thus with himself, 'God, I thank You that I am not like other men—extortioners, unjust, adulterers, or even as this tax collector. I fast twice a week; I give tithes of all that I possess.' And the tax collector, standing afar off, would not so much as raise his eyes to heaven, but beat his breast, saying, 'God, be merciful to me a sinner!' I tell you, this man went down to his house justified rather than the other; for everyone who exalts himself will be humbled, and he who humbles himself will be exalted."
Luke 18: 9–14 (NKJV)

This is getting interesting because Jesus is now equating humble with receiving justification, and not through outward good works. So we have two very different men that the Lord Jesus talks about, one who is a religious Pharisee lifting him- self and the good works that he does, while at the same time putting down another man who was quite the opposite. The other man was a tax collector, a fellow Jew whom Rome has hired to do their dirty work of taxing the pants off Israel. The tax collectors themselves were notorious for skimming off the top for themselves and would never be considered righteous or ever justified in the sight of God because of their evil activities. It would seem obvious if human judgment determined the fate of the two men that the Pharisee would win any argument for righteousness, hands down. Yet Jesus responded with esteem to the man's cry for mercy and gave the truly humble hated tax collector a clean judgment before God, because only this man made himself lower and did not lift himself up. Now the Pharisee went home the same way he came, full of arrogance and superiority for his good works, his true and unrepentant heart was manifested in his prayer, which was full of the filthy sin of pride. The scripture teaches:

For judgment will be merciless to one who has shown no mercy; mercy triumphs over judgment.
James 2:13 (NASB)

God will always show mercy to those who will humble themselves before him, but those who cling to self-righteous- ness and good deeds will not be justified in God's sight. This was the teaching of Jesus about humble. To come before God, you must not come proud or arrogant. You must come humble before him. Today, we people haven't changed much since the days of Jesus. Yes, we have technology and more knowledge than ever, and yes we have many who are doing good, but sometimes with the wrong motivation. What moves the heart of God is found again in the scriptures. Remember anything not done in love will not only be burned up but is just a lot of noise to God.

If I speak with human eloquence and angelic ecstasy but don't love, I'm nothing but the creaking of a rusty gate. If I speak God's Word with power, revealing all his mysteries and making everything plain as day, and if I have faith that says to a mountain, "Jump," and it jumps, but I don't love, I'm nothing If I give everything I own to the poor and even go to the stake to be burned as a martyr, but I don't love, I've gotten nowhere. So, no matter what I say, what I believe, and what I do, I'm bankrupt without love.
1 Corinthians 13:1–7 (THE MESSAGE)

He hath shown thee, O man, what is good; and what the

Lord doth require of thee, but to do justly, and to love mercy, and to walk humbly with thy God Micah 6:8 (WBT)

Jesus taught that salvation didn't come from doing or being good. Jesus also taught that just because you were a son or daughter of Abraham it automatically get you into the pearly gates. This coincided with the teaching of John who taught the people not to just rely on their earthly heritage, but to have a new renewed and kingdom mind-set, which is the heart behind the word "repentance." We love to throw around this word, especially when we feel someone isn't behaving in accordance with our convictions or so we can make sure they know we are more spiritual and sensitive to God than they are. Pride! Pride! Maybe what we're really sensing is our own need to fall on the rock and let our pride be obliterated into such small pieces they will be blown away by God's wind.

Let's look at the teaching of Jesus regarding salvation a little deeper. Let's join Jesus's conversation with a religious leader who quite possibly had a humble heart.

There was a man named Nicodemus, a Jewish religious leader who was a Pharisee. After dark one evening, he came to speak with Jesus. "Rabbi," he said, "we all know that God has sent you to teach us. Your miraculous signs are evidence that God is with you." Jesus replied, "I tell you the truth, unless you are born again, you cannot see the Kingdom of God." "What do you mean?" exclaimed Nicodemus. "How can an old man go back into his mother's womb and be born again?" Jesus replied, "I assure you, no one can enter the Kingdom of God without being born of water and the Spirit. Humans can reproduce only human life, but the Holy Spirit gives birth to spiritual life. So don't be surprised when I say, 'You must be born again.' The wind blows wherever it wants. Just as you can hear the wind but can't tell where it comes from or where it is going, so you can't explain how people are born of the Spirit." "How are these things possible?" Nicodemus asked. Jesus replied, "You are a respected Jewish teacher, and yet you don't understand these things? I assure you, we tell you what we know and have seen, and yet you won't believe our testimony. But if you don't believe me when I tell you about earthly things, how can you possibly believe if I tell you about heavenly things? No one has ever gone to heaven and returned. But the Son of Man has come down from heaven. And as Moses lifted up the bronze snake on a pole in the wilderness, so the Son of Man must be lifted up, so that everyone who believes in him will have eternal life. "For God loved the world so much that he gave his one and only Son, so that everyone who believes in him will not perish but have eternal life. God sent his Son into the world not to judge the world, but to save the world through him. John 3:1–17 (NLT)

Now this teaching to Nicodemus about how one has eternal life has been of great mystery to many just like it seems to mystify Nicodemus. But what is Jesus really teaching? He's teaching about how to receive the kingdom of God and the only way to get it is by somehow having a second birth experience called being born again. This teaching was foreign to Nicodemus, but without much understanding, he kept listening to Jesus. Apparently, something Jesus said must have gotten through because in the book of John it's this man Nicodemus who brings the burial spices to the tomb of Jesus along with another secret disciple, Joseph of

Arimathea. The discourse with Nicodemus is very clear that eternal life must be received by looking at Jesus the way the children of Israel looked at the bronze serpent on the pole in the wilderness. It was only when the people looked at the serpent on the pole that they would receive healing. Jesus himself would be lifted up as a sacrifice on the cross and whoever would look and believe in him would receive eternal life and salvation.

The people went to Moses and said, "We've sinned, for we spoke against the Lord and you. Pray to the Lord so that he will send the snakes away from us." So Moses prayed for the people. The Lord said to Moses, "Make a poisonous snake and place it on a pole. Whoever is bitten can look at it and live." Moses made a bronze snake and placed it on a pole. If a snake bit someone, that person could look at the bronze snake and live.
Numbers 21:7–9 (CEB)

Jesus was referring to this scripture and incident when he said that he must be lifted up and believed in to have eternal life. Again, the eternal life wouldn't be earned, worked for, or even deserved. It would be given as an act of grace for those who knew the secret of making room for it. Today the simplicity of the gospel of grace is muddied by the misunderstanding between the how to get saved and then how a person lives once they are saved. A genuine salvation or conversion can only happen by grace alone through faith in Christ; this is the gospel truth and what the revelation of scripture communicates. It's only after that unmerited and unearned grace is received that grace will teach a person how to now live in the framework and freedom that only grace can provide. Good works can never accomplish ones salvation. In fact, these good works and striving to attain salvation will always be discarded and counted as an accumulating debt in God's sight. Good works will and should be done but not to be saved but because we are saved. As believers, we are ordained to walk in these good works as an ambassador for Christ. Because many have trusted and put an emphasis on works for salvation, it has served as a catalyst of confusion in the church concerning grace.

The only issue God has with exaltation is how and the motive behind the exaltation.

The flip side of that is cheapening grace by not understanding the cost and price of that great gift of grace purchased for all who will receive and live by it. It's the preface of this book that grace is given to the humble, and those who are proud will find themselves being resisted by God and will repel the very grace they need to save them. So in fact, the only way to receive this grace to save is to have a supernatural conversion that begins with seeing Jesus on the cross, cursed by God, bearing my sin and the sin of the world. The reason we have to be born again is because the first time we are born into sin and the second time we are born again free from it. When Jesus went to the cross, he went as a man who lived above any reproach, sin, or inherent iniquity. So when Jesus died and offered himself, it wasn't for any personal sin but to stop the contamination of sin in those who will believe on him. So to really understand what happens when one is born again and to explain what Jesus says to Nicodemus, we must continue to learn more about what Jesus said about humble.

The key to what Jesus is saying about salvation and being born again is actually found in another teaching of Jesus on humble. I want you to see what Jesus's disciples cannot seem to let go of. It's their quest to know who will be the greatest. This isn't the first or last time Jesus will be dealing with this subject. I want to reiterate that the desire for greatness and the desire to be exalted is one that's not only biblical but also something innate in all of us. The desire to be famous, the desire to be wealthy, the desire to be successful isn't evil or wrong. In fact, almost every time in the scriptures that God is received or welcomed above everything, the person will always go higher, it's the upside of down in action. Any time in the scriptures that anyone has an encounter with God, they'll increase and even be exalted.

The only issue God has with exaltation is how and the motive behind the exaltation. If God was against exaltation, the scriptures wouldn't tell us how to be exalted, and Jesus would never teach on the power of humble. Because of our lack of under- standing of what humble is and what it isn't, we tend to think anyone with ambition, goals, and big dreams can't be humble. I don't believe we should beat people up for having desires for greatness and success. In fact, the influx and influence of the waves of technology and media has brought to the surface the desires in us to be recognized and also rewarded for our talents. Again, please don't be condescending to those who take advantage of the technology because a lot of good is coming from it, especially when it's employed by those who understand that God must be above all and the Source of all exaltation and success. The many faceted gifts and talents that are resident in man have been given as a gift of God's grace. When they are seen in that perspective and by always living by the humble principle, these gifts of grace can and will bring Jesus great glory.

The humble principle is "Power is never in my own ability but in God's strength that comes by lowering and humbling myself, intentionally making room for grace."

So what God wants from us is that we always humble ourselves by bowing and lowering ourselves before God, knowing that as we do that we're continually making room and attracting the grace of God into our lives. The more we make room for grace by the humble principle, we'll see as we go lower, that God will always reciprocate and take us higher.

Take a look at these scriptures so we can all be on the same page:

Humble yourselves before the Lord, and he will exalt you.
James 4:10 (ESV)

Humble yourselves therefore beneath the mighty hand of God, so that at the right time He may set you on high.
1 Peter 5:6 (WNT)

So when Jesus was asked about being the greatest, he didn't get angry with those who asked. Did you hear that? I want you to *shama* this truth, that Jesus will never be angry with you for wanting to know or live a life full of greatness and success. I believe that kind of life is available for all believers wherever you live, whatever your culture, and however you were taught. The grace that comes to humble people is no respecter of per- sons, and that's a good thing!

143

You are a son or daughter of God and not a stepchild or an orphan. Your Father is Abba Papa God, and his generosity knows no bounds. In fact, the only limitation will be to those who don't know how to be humble and receive all "Abba" has in store for them. One of my favorite scriptures is:

He who did not spare His own Son, but delivered Him up for us all, how shall He not with Him also freely give us all things? Romans 8:32 (NKJV)

If God was against exaltation, the scriptures wouldn't tell us how to be exalted, and Jesus would never teach on the power of humble.

This scripture helps us focus on Jesus. The most precious thing to God was his firstborn and begotten, yet because of his love for the world, he delivered Jesus up for you and me. God says, *"If I have given My best, My Son whom I love, how can I hold anything that is less from you"* (Romans 8:32, Ken's paraphrased version).

This scripture is so powerful because it points to God's never ending generosity and desire to see us never lacking in any way, shape, or form. The sacrifice of Jesus paid and, yes, overpaid our debt and the penalty of sin. The great exchange is that everything I deserved, Jesus received on the cross and now everything Jesus deserved I receive freely by grace. Hallelujah! Hallelujah! I love to say Grace! Grace! Shalom! Shalom! It reminds me that everything I have isn't because of me but because of Jesus. The mystery of being born again was told to Nicodemus back in John 3, but in order for us to really understand it, we must look deeper into Jesus's teachings. Believe it or not, being born again has to do with humble.

Now please read this:

At that time the disciples came to Jesus, saying, "Who then is greatest in the kingdom of heaven?" Then Jesus called a little child to Him, set him in the midst of them, and said, "Assuredly, I say to you, unless you are converted and become as little children, you will by no means enter the kingdom of heaven. Therefore whoever humbles himself as this little child is the greatest in the kingdom of heaven. Matthew 18:1–4 (NKJV)

Jesus is talking about entering the kingdom of heaven and who is the greatest in the kingdom of heaven. Jesus, without hesitation, points to one who will humble themselves as a child will be the only ones who enter the kingdom. Please let's go to the next chapter together and learn more about this humble child Jesus is talking about.

CHAPTER EIGHT:

Reigning As Child Kings

THERE'S A PROFOUND and I believe hidden truth and revelation in the teachings of Jesus that I believe can cause a humble revolution. Let's look again at what Jesus says when his disciples ask who is the greatest in the kingdom of God?

At that time the disciples came to Jesus, saying, "Who then is greatest in the kingdom of heaven?" Then Jesus called a little child to Him, set him in the midst of them, and said, "Assuredly, I say to you, unless you are converted and become as little children, you will by no means enter the kingdom of heaven. Therefore whoever humbles himself as this little child is the greatest in the kingdom of heaven. Matthew 18:1–4 (NKJV)

The Bible tells us that God doesn't mind us reasoning or using the intellect that he has given us when it comes to God's Word. Just because a truth is unknown or yet to be revealed or understood, does it make it less true? The laws that govern the universe are still being discovered though they've been working for us long before you and I got here.

Just as natural knowledge is greatly increasing as the prophet Daniel spoke, I believe spiritual knowledge and revelation is multiplying at a rapid pace. I love hearing different ministers share their inspiration and revelations whether spoken, in print, or media. All spiritual truth will ultimately be taught by the anointing and teaching of the Holy Spirit, who will take the truth's revealed and plant them in a heart that can receive them. When you hear a truth for the first time, it's the ministry of the Holy Spirit to confirm or affirm that as a Word from God for you. For believers in Christ, any truth that he doesn't make real to you is just the word of a man. When the Holy Spirit quickens or makes that word alive, it changes everything, and it becomes what we call a Rhema, which is a living or spoken word. It's my prayer that the Holy Spirit will make the truths about humble real and alive in your heart and that you'll live differently because of the fresh new truth that you receive.

Jesus responds to his disciples' desire to know how to be great in God's kingdom in a very unique way. Wouldn't you have thought that Jesus would've spoken about one of the great prophets or kings of Israel? Perhaps Jesus would even talk about himself being the greatest. After all, wasn't Jesus the greatest? But Jesus didn't do that. Instead, Jesus takes a little child and puts the child center stage. The Greek word for child here is:

παιδίον paidion
1.   A young child, a little boy, a little girl

a.   Infants
b.   Children, little ones

c.   An infant

We don't know for sure how old the little child was, but for sure, they were very young and most likely too young to discern right from wrong and for sure too young to take care of or raise themselves. So now Jesus answering the question of the greatest says it's a young child. For a moment, just think about how a young child cannot care for himself, he can't teach himself, he most likely can't cook, he can't clean, and he might not even be able to dress himself. So the mere fact that Jesus takes a child and sets him as the greatest in the kingdom shows that greatness in the kingdom has nothing to do with what you can do for or in yourself. A young child is one who must be taken care of by those raising him, usually parents or guardians. Jesus not only tells the disciples that this child, who can hardly do anything but eat, drink, play, and not even go to the bathroom without help, was the greatest in the kingdom of heaven. Jesus doesn't just say the little child is the greatest. He says emphatically that in order for anyone to even enter the kingdom of heaven he has to be converted into a little child like the one he sets in their midst. The very thought of the greatest in the kingdom is a helpless little child and that in order for anyone to enter the kingdom they must be converted into that little child is a profound truth. The word "converted" here is the Greek word:

στρέφω strephō
1.   To turn, turn around
2.   To turn one's self (i.e. to turn the back to one

a.   Of one who no longer cares for another)

b.　　　Metaph. to turn one's self from one's course of conduct,
i.e. to change one's mind

Now Jesus is saying to his disciples, "You must turn back to becoming like children" (Matthew 18:3, web). Jesus then confirms this once more by not only saying that you cannot enter the kingdom unless you turn back to becoming like a little child but also the greatest in the kingdom is one who will humble themselves like this child.

Therefore whoever humbles himself as this little child is the greatest in the kingdom of heaven.
Mathew 18:4 (NKJV)

I believe the two individual truths of converting like a child and humbling himself like the little child isn't two separate truths but a combined truth that brings to light what the power of humble really is. This teaching is also the continuation of the talk Jesus had with Nicodemus about being born again so you can enter the kingdom of God. Jesus teaches in Matthew that you cannot enter the kingdom without this conversion. This is a powerful and profound truth because today we argue about who is really saved and who isn't based usually on something different from the criteria Jesus gives on how to enter the kingdom. Jesus is teaching the disciples how to be great in the kingdom, a desire that was apparently in them in abundance, as well as how no one will enter the kingdom without that turning or conversion into a humble child. The illustration that Jesus was using couldn't be misunderstood or debated by anyone. It's so clear that even a child can and does receive it. Jesus's teaching on humble was a teaching that was for everyone and anyone who would listen. There would be no exclusions or exceptions to getting into the kingdom or greatness in the kingdom. The only way to receive the kingdom was to receive it as a little, humble child.

The only way to receive the kingdom was to receive it as a little, humble child.

One day some parents brought their children to Jesus so he could lay his hands on them and pray for them. But the disciples scolded the parents for bothering him. But Jesus said, "Let the children come to me. Don't stop them! For the Kingdom of Heaven belongs to those who are like these children." And he placed his hands on their heads and blessed them before he left.
Matthew 19:13–15 (NLT)

One day some parents brought their children to Jesus so he could touch and bless them. But the disciples scolded the parents for bothering him. When Jesus saw what was happening, he was angry with his disciples. He said to them, "Let the children come to me. Don't stop them! For the Kingdom of God belongs to those who are like these children. I tell you the truth, anyone who doesn't receive the Kingdom of God like a child will never enter it." Then he took the children in his arms and placed his hands on their heads and blessed them.
Mark 10:13–16 (NLT)

But Jesus called them to Him and said, "Let the little children come to Me, and do not forbid them; for of such is the kingdom of God. Assuredly, I say to you, whoever does not receive the kingdom of God as a little child will by no means enter it." Luke 18:16–17 (NKJV)

I believe we have established, by a multitude of witnesses scripturally, that it is the humble that God will exalt. Also in order for anyone to even enter the kingdom or be great in the kingdom that person must turn and somehow be transformed into a little, humble child. I want to emphasize this especially when it comes to salvation and the promise of eternal life. We sometimes forget that the Judea-Christian religion is one that was always based on God's love and grace and those who would choose to put their trust and rest in what God had freely provided. Jesus identified himself as a Son who put his trust completely in his father. We know that Jesus lived the life completely humble at all times, fully trusting and dependent on the Abba Father.

When Jesus spoke and lived for the most part He spoke to "the lost sheep of the house of Israel."
Matthew 15:24 (NKJV)

It was these lost sheep that had begun to live and believe differently than the humility of the patriarch's in exchange for the pride of the Pharisees. In essence, they had bought the lie of religion, which tells a man he can be good enough or work hard enough to be close to God. Jesus' teaching wasn't about religion but the relationship with a good, loving God that leaves an abundant inheritance to all His children.

The revelation I'm about to share with you I haven't heard from anyone else. If I did hear it from someone else I wouldn't be ashamed or hesitant to share it because I believe it will change your life and perspective when it comes to your relationship with God.

Jesus said more than one time, "Whoever does not receive the Kingdom as a little child will by no means enter it" (Luke 18:17 and Mark 10:15, NKJV).

Because we hear or read with a western mind-set and not in the Jewish mind-set of the people Jesus was primarily teaching, we sometimes miss out on deep, powerful, and perhaps common knowledge to those Jesus was speaking to. Again, me being Jewish and my wife what people call a Ruth (that just means she is a Gentile who loves Jews. Hallelujah!), I know because of our upbringings, my wife and I see God in a different light. She grew up Pentecostal, and I grew up Jewish, so enough said, you get the point!

Now, the first time I saw this revelation was about a year or so ago, and I was blown away. You see Jesus speaking to his fellow Jews, who were brought up to study and learn the Torah and the stories of the Old Testament. When Jesus spoke, they would be filtering what they heard through what they had already read and studied. It's for this reason that when Jesus told the people about the only way to enter the kingdom of God you must receive it as a child, the people would've had a light bulb moment. That just means they would have thought to themselves, "Who in the Old Testament received the kingdom as a child?" Do you know there were two young child kings in Israel's history? One child was a king of Judah, and one child was a king of Israel. So when Jesus taught on receiving the kingdom as a child, their Jewish minds would've taken them back to the two kings who received the kingdom as a child. I hope I have your attention because the first time I saw this God surely had mine.

The two child kings were Josiah and Jehoash. Josiah was eight years old when he became king, and Jehoash was seven years old. Let me ask you a question, would you feel comfort- able if the leader of the nation in which you live was only seven or eight years old? Would you say that a seven or eight year old is qualified in any way to lead anyone, and for that matter, an entire nation? Could God be saying to us that, "In order to receive my kingdom you have to humble yourself and receive my kingdom as a child king who has nothing in his or herself that makes them worthy of receiving such a kingdom"?

The ability a child has to learn, follow, and trust those appointed as teachers is one that comes naturally for the humble child.

Jehoash was 7 years old when he became king.
2 Kings 11:21 (CEB)

Now this Jehoash received the kingdom at seven years old. He began to reign on the throne of Judah as a little child. Sounds familiar? He received the kingdom as a little child just like Jesus said. Now what's interesting in this story is in the details. Let's read on:

He became king in Jehu's seventh year, and he ruled for forty years in Jerusalem. His mother's name was Zibiah; she was from Beersheba. Jehoash always did what was right in the Lord's eyes, because the priest Jehoiada was his teacher.
2 Kings 12:1–2 (CEB)

The key to Jehoash success was that as a humble child king, he was open to the instruction of the priest name Jehoiada who would instruct and train him on how to lead Judah as a child king. Look at the Hebrew word for Jehoiada's teaching:

Instructed : ירה yarah (*The root word for Torah***)**
1.   to throw, cast
2.   to shoot
3.   to point out, show
4.   to direct, teach, instruct
5.   to throw water, rain

The ability a child has to learn, follow, and trust those appointed as teachers is one that comes naturally for the humble child. Unfortunately, as they get older, it's not always the case. So when Jesus is telling about the kingdom being received as a little, humble child, he is referring to kings like Jehoash who is reigning as a child king, yet fully dependent on the wisdom of the teaching priest Jehoiada. This is also how we as child kings who receive God's kingdom are to reign, always humble and fully dependent on the teacher, the Holy Spirit who imparts and teaches us God's Word. Again, as long as Jehoash was listening and following the instruction of Jehoiada as a humble child, Jehoash led Judah as a child king successfully.

So we find Jehoash receiving the kingdom at seven years old for no other reason than he is of royal blood and in the lineage of the king. Oh, by the way, there's such an interesting story in the Bible on how Jehoash became the king at seven in the first place.

When Athaliah, the mother of King Ahaziah of Judah, learned that her son was dead, she began to destroy the rest of the royal family. But Ahaziah's sister Jehosheba, the daughter of King Jehoram, took Ahaziah's infant son, Joash, and stole him away from among the rest of the king's children, who were about to be killed. She put Joash and his nurse in a bedroom to hide him from Athaliah, so the child was not murdered. Joash remained hidden in the Temple of the Lord for six years while Athaliah ruled over the land.
2 Kings 11:1–3 (NLT)

The Jewish mind-set would have related to Jesus's teaching and understood the two kings who received the kingdom as little children.

Athaliah had made herself the queen even though she had no legitimate or legal right to the throne of Judah. She wasn't an heir, but she had stolen the kingdom and was holding onto it with everything she could muster. It was during this time that the rightful heir was hidden in the temple, being taken care of as an infant who was legally and legitimately the king by his royal bloodline. The priest who later instructs Jehoash during his reign understands his purpose and call to set the true king in his place even though the true king is very, very young. It's in the seventh year that Jehoida the priest shows for the first time the royal heir and true king to the leaders and a plan is devised to anoint the young king and remove the false queen Athaliah out. The priest makes a covenant with the people, and they not only kill and remove the evil queen but also remove the

155

altars that she had erected and her priest for Baal rather than the true God Jehovah. This was all done in the name of King Jehoash without his knowledge or approval. It was done for him. He didn't earn it, deserve it, work for it, or even comprehend what was done for him. As a child king, it was only for Jehoash to receive his rightful inheritance. Because we must relate this back to Jesus' teach- ing on receiving the kingdom as a humble child, as it is the same for us who, as humble children of God, don't work, earn, or deserve the greatness of the kingdom our God richly, freely and abundantly bestows on us? Did we receive the kingdom by grace or works? Do we really have a grasp and understanding of the keys of the kingdom that are now ours as we, like Jehoash, are having to depend on our High Priest Jesus and the Holy Spirit to teach us about our inheritance? Doesn't this teaching on receiving the kingdom as a child king mess you up at least just a little bit?

The Jewish or Hebrew mind-set would have related to Jesus's teaching and understood the two kings who received the kingdom as little children. The picture of humble was clearer to them than the church today. Jesus wanted the disciples to know the greatest in the kingdom were the ones who could simply receive their inheritance as a child. An inheritance is usually given when someone dies and leaves to the heirs what the heirs never worked for, earned, or probably deserved. In fact, an inheritance is a gift of pure grace. Those who have been so fortunate to be on the side of the receiving know how humbling that can be. Many times the price that was paid for what is freely passed down through inheritance won't be fully known by the heirs of that inheritance. We know that the grace that we can freely receive isn't without the greatest cost and sacrifice of Jesus to give us what we can't earn, work for, or deserve. Jesus teaches this same truth in the beatitudes as well.

Now when Jesus saw the crowds, he went up a mountain. He sat down and his disciples came to him. He taught them, saying:

"Happy are people who are humble, because they will inherit the earth. (Matthew 5:5)(Matthew 51-2,5, ceb)

The Greek word for **Inherit** is: κληρονομέω klēronomeō

1.   To receive a lot, receive by lot

a.   Esp. to receive a part of an inheritance, receive as an inheritance, obtain by right of inheritance
b.   To be an heir, to inherit

2.   To receive the portion assigned to one, receive an allotted portion; receive as one's own or as a possession
3.   To become partaker of, to obtain

The word translated in many translations, as "meek" is the **Greek word: πραΰς prays** Mildness of disposition, gentleness of spirit, meekness

Meekness toward God is that disposition of spirit in which we accept his dealings with us as good, and therefore without disputing or resisting. In the OT, the meek are those wholly relying on God rather than their own strength to defend against injustice. Thus, meekness toward evil people means knowing God is permitting the injuries they inflict,

157

that he is using them to purify his elect and that he will deliver his elect in his time (Isa 41:17, Luke 18:1–8).

Gentleness or meekness is the opposite to self-assertiveness and self-interest. It stems from trust in God's goodness and control over the situation. The gentle person is not occupied with self at all. This is a work of the Holy Spirit, not of the human will (Gal 5:23)

There is such a fine line between humble and meekness; it's virtually undistinguishable in the Old Testament from the word "humble." In fact, Jesus is actually quoting a scripture from the Old Testament in the beatitudes. Perhaps the best way to describe meekness is "Humble in action or humble living." Again in the Old Testament the same Hebrew word (ענו `-anav) is translated many times as "humble" rather than "meek."

But the meek (ענו -`anav) shall inherit the earth, And shall delight themselves in the abundance of peace.

Psalm 37:11 (NKJV)

The same idea of meek or humble is found in these scriptures:

For the Lord takes pleasure in His people; He will beautify the humble (ענו -`anav) with salvation.
Psalm 149:4 (NKJV)

When God arose to judgment, To save all the humble (ענו-`anav) of the earth. Selah.
Psalm 76:9 (nasb)

158

For the Lord takes pleasure in His people;He will beautify the humble (ענו -`anav) with salvation.
Psalm 149:4 (NKJV)

When you receive the kingdom as a child you don't get what you can do or make happen but what God has abundantly given to you in the form of an inheritance.

There is an important truth and blessing for those who choose to live in humble rather than pride. When we operate in pride, not only does God resist us, but we can only achieve in our own strength and ability. What Jesus teaches in the beatitudes and more intimately to his disciples was that when you receive the kingdom as a child you don't get what you can do or make happen but what God has abundantly given to you in the form of an inheritance. The idea of inheritance is rich throughout the New Testament as well, but more on this later. For now let's look at Josiah and how he received the kingdom and began to reign in Jerusalem at just eight years old.

Josiah was eight years old when he became king, and he reigned in Jerusalem thirty-one years. His mother was Jedidah, the daughter of Adaiah from Bozkath. He did what was pleasing in the Lord's sight and followed the example of his ancestor David. He did not turn away from doing what was right
2 Kings 22:1–2 (nlt)

What was unique about Josiah was more than his reign at eight years old. This child king had been prophesied about three hundred years before he was born as one who would bring spiritual reforms to Israel. So at a very young age, Josiah, though inexperienced in leadership, began to follow the heart and later the Word of God to bring about great reforms as a child king. When Josiah discovered the Torah scroll buried during his restoration he had it read to him. He instantly realized how Israel had been living in great disobedience in not following God's Word. Josiah seeks direction from the prophets and priests, and because of Josiah's ability to stay humble, the impending disaster is upheld to a later time.

This is what the Lord says: I am going to bring disaster on this city and its people. All the words written in the scroll that the king of Judah has read will come true. For my people have abandoned me and offered sacrifices to pagan gods, and I am very angry with them for everything they have done. My anger will burn against this place, and it will not be quenched.' "But go to the king of Judah who sent you to seek the Lord and tell him: 'This is what the Lord, the God of Israel, says concerning the message you have just heard: You were sorry and humbled yourself before the Lord when you heard what I said against this city and its people—that this land would be cursed and become desolate. You tore your clothing in despair and wept before me in repentance. And I have indeed heard you, says the Lord. So I will not send the promised disaster until after you have died and been buried in peace. You will not see the disaster I am going to bring on this city.'"
2 Kings 2:16–22 (NLT)

When it comes to reigning as a child king like Josiah, we must continue to stay humble even after we have been in the trenches, so to speak, awhile. So when Jesus said to receive the kingdom as a child, he knew exactly what and whom he was referring to. He wanted the people to see how powerful and pure humble is displayed when we come as little children. When a child is young, he doesn't know about pride. Unfortunately, he will learn that later. When a child is young, there's an innocence and beauty that's so spectacular! I just love our young kids at church. I love their faith, and I love that they want to do what's right and desire to be good. Those who have been jaded along life's journey do such damage as they take away the innocence, transparency, and vulnerability of our young children, only to corrupt them. It's my heart and prayer that we all go back to the beauty and innocence of being a little child. After all that's the only way to the kingdom. Isn't it time to see real conversion and the turning back to the humble hearts of children for the greatness in God's kingdom?

Let's pray:

Father, make my heart tender and pure as I turn and become again a little child before you. I receive your kingdom now as a little child. Like Jehoash, I keep my ears open to the instruction of my High Priest Jesus and the Holy Spirit who is my teacher. Like Josiah, I keep myself tender and humble, not just today, but throughout my life's journey of faith. I renounce any pride or arrogance and make myself lower as I humble myself before you, Abba Papa God. I intentionally make room for your power, your strength, and most of all your grace as I choose to receive Your kingdom as a humble child. Amen.

CHAPTER NINE:

The Inheritance Only Grace Can Give

Let's NOW CONTINUE on our journey into an aspect of humble that we have briefly touched on in the last chapter but we must not stop now. The revelation that we are child kings and receive our inheritance through grace must be fully uncovered and explored. There are revelations and truth in the Bible that we think we know so we kind of glance or skip past them, thinking we already know that, heard that or "Yeah, yeah enough about that, let's move on." Usually, like a hidden treasure, the Word of God has been buried beneath what the natural eyes can see. As with anything that is hidden, it must be discovered, uncovered, and then finally presented to those who would've never even believed it was hidden in the first place. And so the revelation of living as humble has perhaps been buried for a time like this to prepare and propel us upward and forward from glory to glory.

When someone receives an inheritance, it's because of relationship not because of behavior or works.
Definition of inheritance
a.   The act of inheriting property

b.   The reception of genetic qualities by transmission from parent to offspring
c.   The acquisition of a possession, condition, or trait from past generations
d.   Something that is or may be inherited
e.   tradition
f.   A valuable possession that is a common heritage from nature

When the Bible talks about inheritance, it's always the result of a transfer from one person or generation to another because of either a blood or marriage relationship. The scriptures dealing with inheritance are many. We won't be able to go through each individually. I'll say on the onset that the greatest blessings given by God have always been given because of grace and not works.

Don't pay people back with evil for the evil they do to you, or ridicule those who ridicule you. Instead, bless them, because you were called to inherit a blessing.
1 Peter 3:9 (GWT)

Do you see that you as a believer were called to inherit a blessing? This is the blessing that only grace can give.

And that you should not lose heart, but that you would be imitators of those who by faith and patience have become heirs of The Promise.

Hebrews 6:12 (ARAMAIC BIBLE IN PLAIN ENGLISH)

We must now distinguish between those who receive the inherited blessing and those who will not. Jesus was the first to receive the inherited blessing of his father because he made himself lower by humbling himself lower than any man. The price of humility is nothing in comparison to the glory of the inheritance one can receive when they make room for grace. Unfortunately and rightfully, so those who don't make room for this grace won't receive the inheritance that's been made available to those who are humble. An example of not receiving the inheritance is in the story of Esau.

Looking carefully lest anyone fall short of the grace of God; lest any root of bitterness springing up cause trouble, and by this many become defiled; lest there be any fornicator or profane person like Esau, who for one morsel of food sold his birthright. For you know that afterward, when he wanted to inherit the blessing, he was rejected, for he found no place for repentance, though he sought it diligently with tears.
Hebrews 12:15–17 (NKJV)

Now we know that Esau, the firstborn son of Jacob was in line as the rightful heir to the blessing of inheritance. The bloodline of Esau had secured him the blessing of grace, but he sold that birthright for a plate of food instead. Perhaps Esau thought he would somehow get his birthright and inherited blessing back, but it was too late for that. In the same way, only those that make room for the inherited blessing by humility will receive their rightful inheritance.

If those who are of the law are heirs, faith is made empty
and the promise is canceled.
Romans 4:14 (HCSB)

*When someone receives an inheritance, it's because of
relationship not because of behavior or works.*

What a powerful scripture and the reason why so many of
God's people don't receive the inheritance of grace God has
for them. All the promises of God are given to those who
understand whose they are and who they are in Christ. The
inheritance of grace is given to those who receive the
kingdom as a little child and therefore works has nothing to
do with it, just believing and receiving the simplicity of
God's Word. I want you to see the promises given to us by
inheritance and relationship with Christ.

Christ redeemed us from the curse of the law, having
become a curse for us. For it is written, "Cursed is everyone who hangs on a tree," that the blessing of Abraham
might come on the Gentiles through Christ Jesus; that we
might receive the promise of the Spirit through faith. For
if the inheritance is of the law, it is no more of promise; but
God has granted it to Abraham by promise.

Galatians 3:13, 14, 18 (WEB) For you did not receive a
spirit of slavery to bring you back again into fear; on the
contrary, you received the Spirit, who makes us sons and by
whose power we cry out, "Abba!" (That is, "Dear
Father!").The Spirit himself bears witness with our own
spirits that we are children of God; and if we are children,
then we are also heirs, heirs of God and joint-heirs with the
Messiah.

165

Romans 8:15–17 (CJB) What God has done for you and me has all been done freely through Jesus our Messiah. Every blessing is a blessing of inheritance giving to us freely that has been pre-purchased for us and the blessings of grace and our inheritance is now on a heavenly prepaid debit card. The heart of the Gospel has always been by grace alone and by Christ alone. The only thing we have to do is not work, (trust me I know this is an oxymoron) but we must choose to believe and receive the gift of our inheritance and the blessing that has been given freely by the atoning blood and redemption that makes us connected and joined to Messiah Jesus. Even the angels know that they are now sent to minister for us because we are now the rightful heirs of salvation. Hebrews 1:14 (NKJV)

"And now I entrust you to God and the message of his grace that is able to build you up and give you an inheritance with all those he has set apart for himself.
Acts 20:32 (NLT)

I will deliver you from the Jewish people, as well as from the Gentiles, to whom I now send you, to open their eyes, in order to turn them from darkness to light, and from the power of Satan to God, that they may receive forgiveness of sins and an inheritance among those who are sanctified by faith in Me.
Acts 26: 17–18 (NKJV)

There is no doubt that God wants his people to receive the inheritance of grace that he has so freely provided, yet some- times good people have been misguided by religious teaching that they can't seem to wrap their minds around grace, and they always equate good or bad things happening because of behavior and works. This is especially true in Pentecostal and charismatic circles where grace hasn't been preached out of fear the people will run wild. Although I understand where they are coming from it's not biblically sound doctrine and the lack of teaching on grace keeps the people in a cycle of sin-consciousness rather than the gift of righteousness that Jesus has paid such a price for. The fear tactics, in my opinion, frankly don't work to keep anyone serving or growing in the things of God. I believe only when people truly receive the love that God has for them can they in turn be lovers of God. Another hindrance also found in some circles is the feeling and teaching of unworthiness. This is a form of false humility as well and keeps God's people bound and always looking at self instead of the abundant and glorious provision that comes from looking at Christ and what he alone has provided. As a minister, I see people come from all types of teachings that have formed as deep layers of resistance and strongholds in the mind and keep them from the inheritance of grace Jesus came to give. This is why it's so important to continue to make room for God's grace by staying and clothing ourselves in humility.

Yes, all of you clothe yourselves with humility, to subject yourselves to one another; for "God resists the proud, but gives grace to the humble." Humble yourselves therefore under the mighty hand of God, that he may exalt you in due time; casting all your worries on him, because he cares for you.
1 Peter 5:5B–7 (WEB)

The blessings and inheritance of grace is given to those who are in Christ. These blessings have much to say about his heart and love for us, his beloved. Again, the gift of grace or inheritance isn't saying we deserve or are earning these blessings. These blessings come out of the heart of a humble Jesus who made himself lower so he could ultimately take his people higher and call us to sit with him in heavenly places. Thank God there really is an upside of down!

We have also received an inheritance in Christ. We were destined by the plan of God, who accomplishes every- thing according to his design. The Holy Spirit is the down payment on our inheritance, which is applied toward our redemption as God's own people, resulting in the honor of God's glory. I pray that the eyes of your heart will have enough light to see what is the hope of God's call, what is the richness of God's glorious inheritance among believers. Ephesians 1:11, 14, 18 (CEB)

Right now I'm so excited, and my spirit is jumping because I know I'm getting it and so are you! The inheritance that God gives freely to us is actually confirmed by the presence of the Holy Spirit who comes to live inside every person who is born again. It's also the ministry or career of the Holy Spirit to always remind us of the words of Jesus and confirm his work in us as the Spirit of truth. The Holy Spirit cannot lead you astray from God's Word and truth. He will also affirm you always as God's beloved son or daughter, a receiver of the free blessings of grace and continue to be your comforter, teacher, guide, and friend. It's the Holy Spirit that will also remind you of your inheritance and his ability to keep you until the day Jesus comes again.

God the Father chose you because of what he knew beforehand. He chose you through the Holy Spirit's work of

making you holy and because of the faithful obedience and sacrifice of Jesus Christ. May God's grace and peace be multiplied to you. May the God and Father of our Lord Jesus Christ be blessed! On account of his vast mercy, he has given us new birth. You have been born anew into a living hope through the resurrection of Jesus Christ from the dead. You have a pure and enduring inheritance that cannot perish—an inheritance that is presently kept safe in heaven for you. Through his faithfulness, you are guarded by God's power so that you can receive the salvation he is ready to reveal in the last time.
1 Peter 1:2–5 (CEB)

It's the Holy Spirit that will also remind you of your inheritance!

Now finally I want to leave you with the story of Abraham and how he received his inheritance by believing what God told him. It was Abraham that humbled himself to receive what was impossible to produce in his own ability or strength. Abraham had to learn to trust that the inheritance God would give him would be much greater than anything he could imagine for himself. This is why God took Abraham out to see the stars of the sky and then the sand of the sea as a visual illustration of what Abraham could have with an inheritance from God.

By faith Abraham obeyed when he was called to go out to a place that he was going to receive as an inheritance. He went out without knowing where he was going. By faith he lived in the land he had been promised as a stranger. He lived in tents along with Isaac and Jacob, who were coheirs

of the same promise. He was looking forward to a city that has foundations, whose architect and builder is God.
Hebrews 11:8–10 (CEB)

When this scripture says that Abraham went out it is talking about how Abraham left everything that was familiar including his family, culture, and friends in order to follow and walk before God. The journey was one that took living in the power of the humble principle.
The humble principle is "Power is never in my own ability but in God's strength that comes by lowering and humbling myself, intentionally making room for grace."

The principle of receiving the inheritance of grace is no different for us today. Yet if we insist on cleaving to our own beliefs, culture and even family above the following of God we have chosen and negated the inheritance that can only come from being humble and making room for Christ to give us what no family, culture, or friend can ever do for us.

This is the inheritance that only grace can give and only to those who will be humble enough to receive its great wealth.

For if, because of one man's trespass, death reigned through that one man, much more will those who receive the abundance of grace and the free gift of righteousness reign in life through the one man Jesus Christ.
Romans 5:17 (ESV)

CHAPTER TEN:

Humble Love

THE GRACE THAT brings to us our inheritance is one that is birthed in God's love for his people. It's only when you catch a glimpse of God's love for you that you will not hesitate
to humble yourself and even come boldly before his throne of grace. The comprehension of the love of God is one that doesn't come naturally or understood by our mind or our unredeemed fleshly nature. The love that God has for us has been compared to a mother's love or brother's love, but in reality, there can be no comparison to what the Bible deems the Heavenly Father's agape love for all humanity and for the sons and daughters that have been begotten by that love. Many of us know the scriptures teach this love, but few actually receive the revelation or baptism of that love. Many years ago back in Toronto, there was a revival that was completely birthed and sustained by people who would travel from around the globe and be touched by this love. I still remember being in a service where Bishop Joseph Garlington shared his experience traveling to Toronto where God apprehended him to such an extent that the esteemed bishop spent most of the time in tears and on the floor as

billows of God's love continued to overwhelm him over and over again. Bishop Garlington also shared how he was looking for the revival to be so much different and had no personal expectations of a radical encounter with the love of God. He told the conference how this love forever changed his life and ministry, and we are all the better for it. I can assume that many who will be reading this book have, like the bishop, no real personal encounter with the love of God. They say that a picture is worth a thousand words, but what's a tangible touch and baptism of God's love worth? My journey with the love of God began at the age of fifteen when my dad took me to a charismatic church in Florida where I was living with my mom. (They had been divorced since I was just twelve years old.) To be honest, my experience with that church changed my life. Not only did I grow in my faith, but it was there at just sixteen years old I met the woman who would not long after be my wife. Now, I'm getting a little ahead of myself, but to keep the story short, it was the pastor and youth pastor's message of God's love that really shaped my walk with God. Again, it wasn't just the preaching or the reading of the Word about the love of God but the presence of that divine, heavenly love that wrecked me more than once. Oh, by the way, when I say *"wrecked, wasted, smoked, or smashed,"* it's a good thing, and I don't mean any disrespect. These words are buzzwords to describe what happens when God has apprehended you and flooded you with so much love your body can hardly take it. Before I knew any of those terms, my wife, who had been very hungry for the presence of God and knowing I needed it more than her, devised a plan to take a family vacation that involved somehow stopping at a Virginia campground where Ruth Heflin had her summer meetings going.

Now this was back probably in the late nineties or so, before this powerful woman of God had passed. If you ever get a chance, read any of her books on "glory," do so for they are life-altering. So during our "vacation," we went one night to this open-air tabernacle. It was like stepping back in time. Nothing in my flesh enjoyed what I heard or saw that night, and if it wasn't for my persistent wife, I would've never gone to the altar when Sister Ruth asked for anyone to come for prayer. So I made my way up front and during the altar call there was some song about the river. I made sure I had all my defenses up and stood there like a hard, dead piece of wood. When Sister Heflin came by, she touched me, oh so slightly. I wasn't about to give her a courtesy drop that's common in charismatic circles. I made sure if God was going to touch me it would have to really be him and not some back- woods preacher.

Now, I don't say this to be disrespectful, but to be transparent and let you know that the encounter, I had that night with the love of God I wasn't looking for, nor did I know I needed it so desperately. In fact, years earlier, I had gone to a prophetic conference where a woman spoke a word to me that I had some deep hurts that God wanted to heal. Again, I had so much baggage and wounds on my heart that I didn't think she heard right. I even told my wife, "That woman didn't hear from God. She was definitely not tuned in." So now as I'm standing at the altar on some grass and dirt, Sister Ruth stops and says to me, "Touch! Now just relax like your floating." When she touched me for the second time, I'll try to explain to you what happened. I immediately fell on the floor and got lost in a river of liquid love where, as I lay for what seemed like hours, God began to take me through my whole life of all the times I had been

173

hurt. Some of these hurts were so deep, like the divorce of my parents and the nonsense that followed.

I needed this love that brought healing to every wound and scar. I can still remember the voice of the Lord as I lay under the power of that love and hearing him tell me my mandate and call as a pastor. He told me over and over again, "Love the people!" I heard it again and again, "Ken, love the people!" The experience I had that day is one I will never forget, and I will tell it from time to time, especially because it defines my mandate as a minister of the gospel. It seems all ministers will have a life message, and I believe mine is to love the people. So when I share with you about humble love, it's not from a place of mere book knowledge but rather a life of experiencing God's healing love. Now the reason I say it's healing, and yes, I know it's much more than that, is because I now can talk about my hurts and scars from a place of wholeness and no pain. Seriously, I have no pain regarding my past hurts over my family and life growing up.

It was still the first day of the week. That evening, while the disciples were behind closed doors because they were afraid of the Jewish authorities, Jesus came and stood among them. He said, "Peace be with you." After he said this, he showed them his hands and his side. When the disciples saw the Lord, they were filled with joy. Thomas, the one called Didymus one of the Twelve, wasn't with the disciples when Jesus came. The other disciples told him, "We've seen the Lord! "But he replied, "Unless I see the nail marks in his hands, put my finger in the wounds left by the nails, and put my hand into his side, I won't believe." After eight days his disciples were again in a house and Thomas was with them.

Even though the doors were locked, Jesus entered and stood among them. He said, "Peace be with you." Then he said to Thomas, "Put your finger here. Look at my hands. Put your hand into my side. No more disbelief. Believe!" Thomas responded to Jesus, "My Lord and my God!"
John 20:19–20, 24–28 (CEB)

It's only when love completely heals the wounds that have punctured into the depth of our soul that we will be able to, without hesitation, show how the love of God has healed us.

Now there are a few important truths I want you to grasp from Jesus's encounter with the disciples after the cross and after the resurrection. First of all, Jesus could show them his scars because for Jesus they no longer hurt. He could even talk about them freely and though they didn't ask to see them, Jesus exposes his hands and side and the disciples were filled with joy. Later, Thomas comes in disbelief that it really is Jesus and declares he will not believe unless he gets to put his hands in Jesus's wounded hands and sides. I know sometimes people get mad at Thomas and call him names like Doubting Thomas, but Jesus doesn't rebuke him for asking to see those things. For Jesus, these wounds don't hurt. They've been completely healed. It's only when love completely heals the wounds that have punctured into the depth of our soul that we will be able to, without hesitation, show how the love of God has healed us as well as talk about them without the former pain and hurt that previously was associated with those scars.

The therapy of God's love cannot be underestimated or overstated. In fact, another truth we find here is that one moment in the presence of the love of Jesus causes Thomas to doubt no more. When I was lying on the floor of that open- air tabernacle in a far out place called Ashland, Virginia, I was apprehended by the presence of divine love. I might have made fun of that place at the beginning, but now I appreciate how special it was and how I wish I would've taken more advantage of people like Ruth Heflin who imparted to me such a love. I just realized as I write this chapter that it's not our humble love but Jesus's humble love that will wait patiently until we are ready to receive what he so desires to do for us, yet we won't let him, and yes sometimes we even resist His great love.

The love of God is one that is supernatural. It'll come to you by the Holy Spirit because according to Romans 5:5, it's the Holy Spirit who will pour God's love upon us. I believe that real love is always passionately pursuing and contending for what only God's grace in our lives can bring us.

I pray that from his glorious, unlimited resources he will empower you with inner strength through his Spirit. Then Christ will make his home in your hearts as you trust in him. Your roots will grow down into God's love and keep you strong. And may you have the power to understand, as all God's people should, how wide, how long, how high, and how deep his love is. May you experience the love of Christ, though it is too great to understand fully? Then you will be made complete with all the fullness of life and power that comes from God. Ephesians 3:16–19 (NLT)

When you know that God loves you, it's easy to walk in humble love and never feel the need to lift yourself, promote yourself, praise yourself, or push yourself.

The Apostle Paul was a man who gave the church the revelation of the gospel of grace. Grace is always underserved, unearned, and unmerited favor that comes only by and through the person of Jesus Christ. The apostle knew that in order for us to receive the revelation of grace, it would begin with first allowing God's love to be rooted deep within our hearts and only from that firm foundation and experience of love would we be filled with the full- ness that only God's love can give. Since we know that it's only love the Bible says never fails, it's the force of God's love that we must know is always holding us. We must learn to be like the Apostle John whose life was radically transformed by Jesus love for him. It was John known as the beloved disciple that knew Jesus love for him who put his head on the breast of Jesus so John could always hear the heartbeat of Jesus.

It's John who more than any disciple writes about his personal experience with Jesus and four times calls himself the disciple whom Jesus loved in the book of John, which of course he penned. When you know that God loves you, it's easy to walk in humble love and never feel the need to lift yourself, promote yourself, praise yourself, or push yourself. Humble love doesn't do any of these things. One of the things that the Apostle Paul says is that love isn't proud. So if love isn't proud, what is love? The opposite or reciprocal of proud is to be humble. This is why Jesus, who is the manifestation of love and the fullness of God's grace,

177

had no problem living in humble love before his Father. Jesus knew he was loved as God verbally and publicly affirmed that love at Jesus's baptism where God said that Jesus was his beloved Son, and he was well pleased by him. By the way, this was before Jesus started his ministry, so God's pleasure had nothing to do with Jesus's performance but rather the relationship of Son with the Father. The next time God expressed his love for Jesus is found here.

While he was saying this, a cloud came and overshadowed them; and they were fearful as they entered the cloud. And a voice came out of the cloud, saying, "This is My beloved Son. Hear Him!" Luke 9:34–35 (NKJV)

Now if we were reading this in the Hebrew you would see not only God affirm his love for his Son Jesus but also for the disciples to *shama* (hear) Jesus, which means they should listen, heed, follow, and obey Jesus as they would the Torah.

The love that Jesus received from his Father is what allowed Jesus to always live in humble love and obedience to his Father. For in the love of God is stability and foundation that provides the safety and security that we all crave. Without this love, we feel exposed, insecure, and must always strive or do something rather than just humbly receive the love God desperately desires to freely give you, which only leads to further emptiness and hurt. An experience or revelation with love, in my opinion, will always be the best teacher. The other night, I watched a show on the OWN network where Lenny Kravitz was sharing his life story. In the segment called "**GRACE**," Lenny describes growing up being part of a boys' choir in

California where one night something happened to him that would change his life forever.

A boy who was rooming with Lenny asked him if he ever heard about Jesus Christ and the love that Jesus had for him. During the conversation with that young boy, Lenny described a holy presence that came into the room and filled it with liquid love. He said, "Both of us felt it as God came in the room and met us with his love." Lenny prayed and asked Jesus to be his Lord and said he never needed any further explanation of God's love. He experienced the presence of Jesus' amazing love, and Lenny Kravitz was forever changed by it. May any- one who reads this book have an experience and encounter with the love of God that is so real and authentic, it can never be denied. *May your love encounter with Jesus begin right now*! **Amen.**

CHAPTER ELEVEN:

No Vacancy!

BECAUSE GRACE IS never earned, deserved, or merited there might be a tendency to think that there's nothing that a per- son can do to either repel or attract that grace. After all, grace is free right? Well, to be quite honest just because something is free doesn't mean you will get to enjoy it or partake of it. For instance, salvation is a free gift, available and purchased for all mankind, but does that make all men automatically saved? Of course not! That false thinking has given birth to universalism, which says there is no need for you and me to repent and believe the gospel of Jesus. So now, if you die, you're automatically received by God into glory without even believing the good news. It also cheapens the blood of Jesus, in my opinion. The Holy Scriptures are clear about the availability of salvation as a gift of grace that must be believed and received by faith. The availability of grace does not necessitate its potent flow into our lives.

I like to describe salvation as a gift. I don't know about you, but I am a gift person. (That just means I just like to receive gifts!) A gift, when it is given, is a wonderful thing, but there's what I like to call the three Rs when it comes to receiving gifts in order for them to be enjoyed. A gift must first be recognized as a gift that's for you. When you recognize a gift, you are accepting the fact that the gift is for you. Then you are ready to receive it. A gift that is not first recognized or received or taken will do no one any good though the gift can be in fact awesome, like the gift of eternal life. Receiving a gift means that you unwrap it and receive what has been given to you. Finally, you must respect the gift by being thankful and appreciate the value of its benefits. Without a true and genuine respect for the gift, it will very soon be discarded for something else. In the book of Isaiah, the Bible says:

"Is anyone thirsty? Come and drink—even if you have no money! Come, take your choice of wine or milk—it's all free! Why spend your money on food that does not give you strength? Why pay for food that does you no good? Listen to me, and you will eat what is good. You will enjoy the finest food "Come to me with your ears wide open. Listen, and you will find life. I will make an everlasting covenant with you. I will give you all the unfailing love I promised to David."
Isaiah 55:1–3 (NLT)

The three "R's"
*   *Recognize*
*   *Receive*
*   *Respect*

Do you see how generous God is? God says come and eat of the finest, and you don't have to pay anything; it's all for free, given by God's grace. I just love how God is willing to give the best of everything to anyone, and it's all for free. Amen? This scripture correlates with the teaching of Jesus in John 10. He tells the people the reason for his coming was to give "life and life more abundantly." The availability of God's grace is for all but without benefit as long as there is a "No Vacancy" sign that resists and repels the grace from moving in. It's only when we stay humble before God that the sign will not appear. When we're humble before God, we're saying to God that we're coming to the table with ears and hearts that shama. In fact, Isaiah 55 says, "Please come ready to 'shama,' to hear, listen, follow and obey." In fact, this is another example of the word 'shama' being repeated twice (שמע shama– שמע shama), so you can come and eat to the full what is truly good and abundant! I can picture God throwing a party, sending out invitations, and then rejoicing when those who make room for grace enjoy the riches of God's grace.

The availability of grace does not necessitate its potent flow into our lives.

The Bible speaks of Noah finding grace in the eyes of the Lord (Genesis 6:8). Could it be that Noah made room for grace and was humble, willing to *shama* and really hear and follow God no matter how crazy that would seem? Did you know that even Noah's name tells us something about him? In the Hebrew the name, נח **Noach** means "rest." Could it be that Noah operated in the principle of humble and that is why grace was attracted to him? Perhaps Noah never had that "No Vacancy" sign up but instead had a sign that said "Room for Grace Always Available!" By the way, Ruth learned that by lying down and lying at the feet of Boaz, she got so much more than working in the fields. Yes, we too will always get much more by lying down and resting in God's presence than working in His fields.But that is also another story and another book!

The humble principle is "Power is never in my own ability but in God's strength that comes by lowering and humbling myself, intentionally making room for grace."

We must be more like Noah who attracted rather than repelled grace. I want to reiterate how dangerous and deceptive pride is for the believer in Christ. The moment we lift our own ability and strength, we become prideful. The definition of prideful is "full of pride." This means a "No Vacancy" sign is already erected, as there's no room for grace. Here are some words from the dictionary related to "prideful."

Synonyms:

Disdainful, haughty, highfalutin (also hifalutin), lofty, lordly, proud, superior

Antonyms:

Humble, lowly, modest Related Words:
Complacent, conceited, egoistic, egotistic (also egotistical), important, self-assertive, self-conceited, self-contented,

self-important, self-satisfied, smug, uppity, vain, vainglorious; arrogant, pretentious, sniffy, snobbish, stuck-up, supercilious; cavalier, overbearing, overweening, peremptory, swaggering; high-sounding, pompous; condescending, patronizing; cocky, overconfident, presuming, presumptuous; bloated, boastful, bombastic, self-glorifying; audacious, bold, brash, brassy, cheeky, cocksure, forward, impertinent, impudent, saucy; confident, presuming, self-assured, self-confident, sure; bossy, domineering, high-handed, imperious; egocentric, self-centered, selfish; dominating, magisterial, masterful

I believe we've established that grace comes or is attracted to those who are humble (James 4:6). I want you to see that it's only by the goodness and abundance that grace provides that has brought you to where you are right now. Because of that simple and yet profound truth we should never be prideful.

Right now, brothers and sisters, the best thing I can do for you is to apply these principles to the situation with Apollos and me. Maybe we can show you the meaning of the saying, "not beyond the things written." If you learn that, perhaps none of you will swell with pride because you fall into the seductive trap of pitting one against the other. Is there any reason to consider yourselves better than others? What do you have that you didn't receive? If you received it as a gift, why do you boast like it is something you achieved on your own?
1 Corinthians 4:6–7 (VOICE)

184

Did you catch what Paul is teaching us by the inspiration of the Holy Spirit? Nothing a man has received he can take credit for or boast about in fact everything a man has received has been given to him as a gift from heaven. The Apostle Paul affirmed this by saying another time, "By the grace of God I am what I am" (1 Corinthians 15:10). He tells the people plainly not to boast and never lift yourself or anyone else up. He was saying, "Please don't get prideful!" Consider some other words of the apostle of grace:

For through the grace given to me I say to everyone among you not to think more highly of himself than he ought to think; but to think so as to have sound judgment, as God has allotted to each a measure of faith.
Romans 12:3 (NASB)

We too will always get much more by lying down and resting in God's presence than working in His fields.

For it's by God's grace that you have been saved. You receive it through faith. It was not our plan or our effort. It is God's gift, pure and simple. You didn't earn it, not one of us did, so don't go around bragging that you must have done something amazing. For we are the product of His hand, heaven's poetry etched on lives, created in the Anointed, Jesus, to accomplish the good works God arranged long ago. Ephesians 2:8, 9 (VOICE)

For I am the least of the apostles and not even fit to be called an apostle because I persecuted God's church. But by God's grace I am what I am, and his grace shown to me was

185

not wasted. Instead, I worked harder than all the others—not I, of course, but God's grace that was with me.
1Corinthians 15:9–10 (ISV)

Could it be possible that the Apostle Paul operated in the humble principle, continually lowering himself before God and therefore making room for grace? I believe when we fail to make room for grace we're holding up a "No Vacancy" sign, and we tell God, "Sorry, but there's no room for you here. I've got this!" It's only when we are like David who only boasted in God that God's abundant and overflowing grace comes to the humble.

There's another powerful scripture of grace abounding to those who make room for it. It's found in the context of those who have learned how to live in the power of generosity.

But this I say: He who sows sparingly will also reap sparingly, and he who sows bountifully will also reap bountifully. So let each one give as he purposes in his heart, not grudgingly or of necessity; for God loves a cheerful giver. And God is able to make all grace abound toward you, that you, always having all sufficiency in all things, may have an abundance for every good work.
2 Corinthians 9:6–8 (NKJV)

The prideful, stingy, and the insecure will never understand the blessing that comes when love flows out of your life in the form of unrestrained generosity. Sad to say, but statistically, the people who have the most will generally give the leastunless they have been forever hooked and smitten with the joy of giving. After all Jesus said:

In all things I gave you an example, that so laboring you ought to help the weak, and to remember the words of the Lord Jesus, that he himself said, "It is more blessed to give than to receive." Acts 20:35 (WEB)

The act of giving is an act that imitates God's grace. It's also in this grace of giving that the apostle wants all of us to abound.

Grace is attracted to the humble givers who trust in God's provision and not their own abilities to provide or sustain themselves.

But as you abound in everything—in faith, in speech, in knowledge, in all diligence, and in your love for us—see that you abound in this grace also.
2 Corinthians 8:7 (NKJV)

According to the scriptures, the heart that will be humble enough to give generously will always have abundance for every good thing God wants them to walk in. God's grace is attracted to those humble enough to realize that everything they have comes from God. It's these people who, when their humble hearts are moved to give, it will only make room for more grace. In fact, the very statement that "God is able to make all grace abound toward you" (2 Corinthians 9:7) tells me that grace is attracted to the humble givers who trust in God's provision and not their own abilities to provide or sustain themselves. This is another way to intentionally go lower that will eventually take you higher! I don't know about you, but I want to make room for "All Grace" to abound in my life. We must remove the "No

Vacancy" in our lives, and choose not to buy into the lie of greed and selfishness that has caused such a small percentage of Christians to handle their financial resources as somehow a distinct and separate part of their lives. This disconnect can only solidify Jesus's warning of those who trust in riches will not enter into the kingdom of God. Again their pride is repel- ling and resisting God's grace with the sign **"No Vacancy!"**

Grace is attracted to the humble givers who trust in God's provision and not their own abilities to provide or sustain themselves.

Teach those who are rich in this world not to be proud and not to trust in their money, which is so unreliable. Their trust should be in God, who richly gives us all we need for our enjoyment. Tell them to use their money to do good. They should be rich in good works and generous to those in need, always being ready to share with others. By doing this they will be storing up their treasure as a good foundation for the future so that they may experience true life.
1 Timothy 6:17–19 (NLT)

Making room for grace means we make a place for the presence of God the way David said, "I need to bring the Ark back to Jerusalem." Now the Ark of God represents the presence of God. It's not the only thing it represents, but for sure, if the Ark was present, God showed up in glory as well. The story of David bringing the Ark back to Jerusalem and then building a tent for it is such a story of the power of humble.

Big doors always swing on little hinges!

I believe humble people will do some things other people might find peculiar or difficult to understand, and still others might say those people are just weird. Over the years, those people who have made room for grace, and God's presence are the same people that, though man rejects, grace is attracted to. Many times people miss out on the greatest blessings in their lives because they judge the book unworthy before opening a single page. I teach my people at Save the Nations, "Don't judge anyone you meet based on mere outward appearance." I can testify that most of the people we tend to reject are sent by God to give us some- thing we will miss because we don't understand the culture of honoring and making room for the gift that God wants to bestow upon us through them. Please remember that big doors always swing on little hinges, like the little maid girl that gave hope to a heathen king so his servant Naaman could not only be healed by grace but also convert to the God of Israel.

Saul was the king before David that was prideful and never saw the need to get the Ark and bring it to Jerusalem during his reign. David brings the Ark back to Jerusalem but not before it makes a short pit stop at the home of Obed-Edom where the Ark is left after a David attempts to bring the Ark back without the divine order of the priesthood carrying the Ark on their shoulders. Instead, mimicking the Philistines, a cart is used to carry the Ark, only to see Uzzah die in a breach before the Lord when he tries to keep the Ark from tilting on some rough ground. Let's pick up with David's second attempt to bring the Ark to the place David has made ready.

The ark of God remained in Obed-Edom's house for three months; the Lord blessed Obed-Edom's family and everything that belonged to him. 1 Chronicles 13:14 (NET BIBLE)

Making room for grace means we make a place for the presence of God!

Because Obed-Edom made room for the Ark of God, the Bible says that everything and everyone who associated with Obed-Edom was blessed. I believe this is a picture of a person who doesn't have the "No Vacancy" sign anywhere to be found. This is a picture of the humble person who makes room for grace. It is grace that will always bless you more than you deserve when you make room for the Ark of God's presence. Do you know that Obed-Edom is a Gittite, from the same town of Gath, where the giant that David killed, was born? Is it possible that God will bless anyone who humbles himself and makes room for him, even the sinner? What an illustration of how the upside of down is available to anyone, yes anyone, who will intentionally go lower before God.

The Lord spoke to me though this story and told me that if we would only make room for the presence of God in our lives like Obed-edom, everything would be blessed. He showed me how we need to make room in relationships and marriages for God's presence, and they would be blessed. As we make room for the presence of God in our careers and finances, they too would be blessed. Then the Lord showed me that the churches that would make room for the presence of God would be blessed and not have to worry about anything else, that God would bless them abundantly. Let's read the story:

Then King David was told, "The Lord has blessed Obed-edom's household and everything he has because of the Ark of God." So David went there and brought the Ark of God from the house of Obed-edom to the City of David with a great celebration. After the men who were carrying the Ark of the Lord had gone six steps, David sacrificed a bull and a fattened calf. And David danced before the Lord with all his might, wearing a priestly garment. So David and all the people of Israel brought up the Ark of the Lord with shouts of joy and the blowing of rams' horns. But as the Ark of the Lord entered the City of David, Michal, the daughter of Saul, looked down from her window. When she saw King David leaping and dancing before the Lord, she was filled with contempt for him. They brought the Ark of the Lord and set it in its place inside the special tent David had prepared for it.

And David sacrificed burnt offerings and peace offerings to the Lord. When he had finished his sacrifices, David blessed the people in the name of the Lord of Heaven's Armies. Then he gave to every Israelite man and woman in the crowd a loaf of bread, a cake of dates, and a cake of raisins. Then all the people returned to their homes.
2 Samuel 6:12–19 (NLT)

David stayed humble and made a place for the Ark and presence of God. Do you know in the last days the scriptures teach that it's this humble tent that God will restore? This is the tent of those who will keep themselves humble and place a value on the presence of God and the grace of Jesus. By the way, it was Obed-Edom and his family who, when the Ark came to Jerusalem, decided to stay with the Ark as doorkeepers according to 1 Chronicles 15:24. I guess when we humble ourselves and make room for grace we'll never be satisfied without the presence of God being near.

For a day in Your courts is better than a thousand. I would rather be a doorkeeper in the house of my God Than dwell in the tents of wickedness. For the Lord God is a sun and shield; The Lord will give grace and glory; No good thing will He withhold From those who walk uprightly. O Lord of hosts, Blessed is the man who trusts in You!
Psalm 84:10–12 (NKJV)

The upside of down is available to anyone, yes anyone, who will intentionally go lower before God.

CHAPTER TWELVE:

The Humble Church

THE CHURCH OF the last hundred years has lost so much credibility. I'm talking about the American Christian church. I'm not pointing the finger at one particular group, association, or denomination. The general consensus or trend in America is one that says, "I love Jesus, just not church or religion." This separation of the Lord and the body he died for and loves is "an inconvenient truth" that few want to discuss and even fewer want to tackle. The fact of the matter is, people do want spirituality and closeness to God. You can see this plainly in the American culture. They also want to know about supernatural things and possibilities, and yet they don't want church. So the trend that we are seeing with people of all ages is "less church" while continuing to look for ways to serve, give back, and demonstrate a social justice gospel. Why is this happening? Why are people leaving the organized and religious institutions to follow what they believe in their hearts God wants them to do? I believe part of this phenomena and the reality of a culture not only leaving the church but also bashing and berating church is because of what the church has been exhibiting for quite some time. Now, we can trace the history of the church back to the day of Pentecost and know that, although there has been many great church movements and leaders, she has also been plagued by those who led the church in a quest for power, money, and fame—the very same sins Satan tried to tempt Jesus with and the same ones the Apostle John warns us of.

It's now the new normal to expect our leaders and the ones we elected to serve to do the opposite of what they say or have promised.

Don't fall in love with this corrupt world or worship the things it can offer. Those who love its corrupt ways don't have the Father's love living within them. All the things the world can offer to you—the allure of pleasure, the passion to have things, and the pompous sense of superiority—do not come from the Father. These are the rotten fruits of this world. This corrupt world is already wasting away, as are its selfish desires. But the person really doing God's will—that person will never cease to be.
1 John 2:15–17 (VOICE)

The corruption in the church has gone many times without the proper and needed response from leaders within the church, which then only solidifies and confirms the beliefs of the masses that church is hypocritical and filled with the fake and the phony, so we must deem it no longer relevant or needed, especially when it comes to true spirituality. As a pastor, I find the skepticism of people and the disrespectfulness and lack of trust in the church frustrating, to say the least. I do my best not to feed into the stereotypes and mind-sets that have been downloaded into people before they have met me or experienced our church, Save the Nations. I like to think of my church as an "unchurch," sort of like 7 Up who marketed and advertised their product as the "Uncola."

So during my short time in church, now about thirty-five years, I have seen the increasing distrust of not only spiritual leaders but especially the political leaders. It's now the new normal to expect our leaders and the ones we elected to serve to do the opposite of what they say or have promised. The spin doctors have become experts in making us forget or so confuse us with the poisonous Kool-Aid that we are too tired or perplexed to sift through the madness. So now when you look at the scandalous history of the church and political figures which seems to be running neck and neck in their hypocrisy and lack of humble, is it any wonder we are perhaps going to have a revolution in order for there to be authentic change? A revolution happens when a people, usually with little or no power, choose to confront and overthrow the current sys- tem with a new or transformed and greatly needed shift. Since revolution usually hap- pens from the ground up, it takes some time for it to be birthed and break through the attitudes, fears, and complacency of those who complain knowing that something needs to be done, but who don't want the upheaval and chaos that comes with a revolution. Eventually the old, deteriorating walls that imprison and confine will come down. The Berlin wall was torn down by people because the pain of living with the wall became greater than the fear of communism's reprisal for removing it. Until the pain is greater than the fear, people for the most part will avoid change no matter how badly it's needed or wanted.

Until the pain is greater than the fear, people for the most part will avoid change no matter how badly it's needed or wanted.

What we have now inbreeded in the culture of society, and even church is the dearth of humble leadership and the profusion of the hypocritical, proud, and the arrogant.

The prophets give false prophecies, and the priests rule with an iron hand. Worse yet, my people like it that way! But what will you do when the end comes?
Jeremiah 5:31 (NLT)

Do you see that God tells Jeremiah that his people love to hear lies rather than truth and to be dominated by false, self-serving leaders? This is just one of many scriptures depicting such horrors.

Those who are arrogant and prideful will not even have the ability to hear the truth that can make them free. The God that loved Israel is the same God that warned them not to let that pride bring them down.

Listen and pay attention. Don't be too proud, because the Lord has spoken to you. Give glory to the Lord your God before he brings darkness and before you slip and fall on the dark hills. You hope for light, but he will turn it into thick darkness; he will change it into deep gloom. If you don't listen to him, I will cry secretly because of your pride. I will

cry painfully, and my eyes will overflow with tears, because the Lord's people will be captured.
Jeremiah 13:15–17 (NCV)

A humble church will most likely come from a revolution, away from the fear of the reprisal of the proud, into the arms of the humble shepherds of love and grace.

Be of the same mind toward one another. Do not set your mind on high things, but associate with the humble. Do not be wise in your own opinion.
Romans 12:16 (NKJV)

Wouldn't it be much better to spend time fostering relationships with those who live in the power of humble rather than in the power of pride? Do you realize that it's the humble that will inherit the earth, not the proud? Those whose quest for power and jockey for position will inherit the wind. The humble church is a new kind of church with renovated and transformed leadership who understand the people are not there to serve them, but they are there to serve and love the people. We should take a lesson from the king who refused to listen to wise counsel of loving, speaking good, and serving the people and ended up with a rebellion on his hands because he refused to lead humbly. Then King Rehoboam consulted the elders who stood before his father Solomon while he still lived, and he said, "How do you advise me to answer these people?" And they spoke to him, saying, "If you will be a servant to these people today, and serve them, and answer them, and speak good words to them, then they will be your servants forever" (1 Kings 12:6-7 NKJV)

The humble church is a new kind of church with renovated and transformed leadership who understand the people are not there to serve them, but they are there to serve and love the people.

The boastful and proud ways of doing church and even politics, I believe, will have a revolution and will bring us back to the purity and possibilities of those who make room for grace by living in the principle of humble.

The humble principle is, "Power is never in my own ability but in God's strength that comes by lowering and humbling myself, intentionally making room for grace."

The humble church will be a church that does more than the social justice aspects of the gospel. The humble church will help to restore the blessing of honor, which opens the door for a revival that releases the power of the gospel to and through the humble.

A man's pride will bring him low, But a humble spirit will obtain honor.
Proverbs 29:23 (NASB)

When Jesus walked the earth He dealt with a man who did much good, but would not humble himself to follow Jesus and deal with the greed in his heart. He was full of religion, yet his real god was his possessions.

As he went out into the street, a man came running up, greeted him with great reverence, and asked, "Good Teacher, what must I do to get eternal life?" Jesus said,

"Why are you calling me good? No one is good, only God. You know the commandments: Don't murder, don't commit adultery, don't steal, don't lie, don't cheat, honor your father and mother." He said, "Teacher, I have—from my youth—kept them all!" Jesus looked him hard in the eye—and loved him! He said, "There's one thing left: Go sell whatever you own and give it to the poor. All your wealth will then be heavenly wealth. And come follow me." The man's face clouded over. This was the last thing he expected to hear, and he walked off with a heavy heart. He was holding on tight to a lot of things, and not about to let go.
Mark 10:17–22 (MESSAGE)

The culture of greed, which includes the cares of this world, has slowly but surely sidled into the lives of God's church and his people. The leaven of worldliness and the little foxes have crept in and are causing the church to lose her influence and relevance in society. We need to get back to a humble people and a humble church that makes room for God to bring genuine revival rather than just a performance or what some now now call Spiritainment!

A lack of honor has come to and through church and political figures because of the root of pride that is seen in greed, cronyism, and narcissism so blatant today. It's only when leaders renounce these things and embrace their weak- ness rather than strength will God's grace be unleashed and great change come.

The humble church will help to restore the blessing of honor, which opens the door for a revival that releases the power of the gospel!

If you're like me, you're getting embarrassed and tired of those, like David, who have given the ammunition for his enemies to speak negatively about God.

However, because by this deed you have given occasion to the enemies of the Lord to blaspheme, the child also that is born to you shall surely die. 2 Samuel 12:14 (NASB)

I believe, despite the negativity and controversy that has been prevalent in the church, we do have a promise of what happens when God's people will humble themselves. Thank God there still is an upside of down! It's not the naysayers, but the remnant that will join the humble revolution and see the reformation and blessing that comes to those who make room for grace when they make themselves humble before God. This also means the church and her leaders will have to apologize to those she has offended and hurt by her refusal to admit and confront the mistakes and even atrocities committed or condoned by leadership of the past. The church must never be too proud or boastful of her position. Instead she must embrace her function as the one who has been given the great task and great commission of reconciling the world back to God. As ambassadors from another world, we must live in this foreign country with hearts of humility and respect for all.

As ambassadors from another world, we must live in this foreign country with hearts of humility and respect for all.

If My people who are called by My name will humble themselves, and pray and seek My face, and turn from their wicked ways, then I will hear from heaven, and will forgive their sin and heal their land.
2 Chronicles 7:14 (NKJV)

Finally, the humble church cannot be afraid to get their hands dirty or be afraid of controversy or the ramifications of doing what is right simply because it's the right thing to do. The confusion of what's right is cleared up in the words of Jesus in what we call the golden rule, which is, "Do unto others, as you would have them do unto you."

So whatever you wish that others would do to you, do also to them, for this is the Law and the Prophets.
Matthew 7:12 (ESV)

Jesus shared a great parable, which demonstrated how far the religious had gone away from what God had intended for Israel. I suppose unless a new humble church arises, we will not be much different. Then Jesus answered and said: "A certain man went down from Jerusalem to Jericho, and fell among thieves, who stripped him of his clothing, wounded him, and departed, leaving him half dead. Now by chance a certain priest came down that road. And when he saw him, he passed by on the other side. Likewise a Levite, when he arrived at the place, came and looked, and passed by on the other side. But a certain Samaritan, as he journeyed, came where he was. And when he saw him, he had compassion. So he went to him and bandaged his wounds, pouring on oil and wine; and he set him on his own animal, brought him to an inn, and took care of him. On the next day, when he departed, he took out two denarii, gave them to the innkeeper, and said to him, 'Take care of him; and whatever more you spend, when I come again, I will repay you.' So which of these three do you think was neighbor to him who fell among the thieves?" And he said, "He who showed mercy on him." Then Jesus said to him, "Go and do likewise." (Luke 10:30-37 NKJB)

The story of the Good Samaritan in the gospel of Luke 10 depicts two religious men, a Levite and a priest, walking in indifference to a man who was visibly hurting. The man was left for dead after thieves had robbed, and attacked him which left him wounded, penniless and almost dead. Only a Samaritan stopped and did the right thing. He helped the man to a place of recovery at his own expense. Jesus told the man who wanted eternal life to do what this Samaritan did for whom Jesus called his neighbor. The Samaritan didn't need a title or a position. He didn't need recognition or remuneration. He had compassion on someone who was hurting and did something about it. We who are the humble church, let's do the same!

Do not withhold good from those who need it, when you have the ability to help.
Proverbs 3:27 (NET BIBLE)

My Upside of Down Journey

A$_S$ I'M WRITING this chapter as the last thing I will
share about the Upside of Down, I'm not sure where this
chapter actually belongs in the order of the book. Do I put
this at the beginning, at the end, or somewhere in between?
I wanted to share with the readers of this book my journey
and my story, which has help to lead me to write this book
and share these thoughts and truth's about the supernatural
power of those who will embrace the principle of humble
and the Upside of Down life to its fullest capacity. Like
many truth's until they are fleshed out they are merely
principles or words on a page. When they are applied,
activated and really lived it changes the words into a
lifestyle that is experienced? It is not enough just to have a
"head" knowledge. We must learn how to live daily in the
power of this "technology for the soul". Because I feel this
is most likely my life message, I can assure you I have had
to humble myself before God a multitude of times, in some
very trying and telling circumstances. Because I believe
these principles are not only biblical but essential to healthy

and authentic living, I want to make myself vulnerable by revealing my upside of down journey which has many times been not only hard and difficult but also healing and rewarding. The tension and so often the time between the two reveal the depth of our true character and the real condition of the heart. The Upside of Down life will feel and look sometimes like you are only going down and never up. Like so many that went before, you must trust that God sees and has your back and eventually the tide will turn and you will be at the higher place that is promised to all who intentionally lower and humble themselves before God. Many times there will be a process and price of you dying to yourself and even to the dreams you once had. When all seems lost and the dream is dead remember the God who confirmed the Messsiah Jesus by the resurrection from the dead. Sometimes what looks like death is merely an opportunity for a resurrection and a new and brighter beginning. You are in good company with people like Moses, Abraham, David, Paul and Jesus, so please don't grow faint, give up or lose heart now. The Upside of Down is that intentionally going lower will take you higher in the end.

As you might already know, I grew up Jewish born in Long Island, New York. My multiethnic roots run deep with a heritage that includes, Russia, Ukraine, Poland, and Romania. The story of my family's salvation can only be explained by and through the grace of God. There is no other explanation that could result in this completely and forever Jewish boy pastoring, preaching, singing, and writing books about Yeshua-Jesus. I want to give honor to my Dad and step-mom who loved me and led me to The

Lord. My dad and grandfather had gotten radically saved through a ministry called "Full Gospel Businessmen" in the late 70's. Now when I tell you radical, these are not just words on a page. My grandparents were deep into new age and searching for truth. My dad was unfulfilled in relationships even though a successful businessman. I can still remember seeing the change in him as I watched him fall in love with Jesus which changed him and me forever. I might have forgot to mention that my mom and her new hus- band have also found Yeshua as their Messiah and have been burning with a passion to reach Jewish people through there ministry in Orlando called Geshur Shalom. This is another Upside of Down story for another time and another book.

When I got saved and met my Yeshua/Jesus Messiah at fifteen, I was blessed to be in the midst of an amazing church that emphasized the love of God and the power of God's Word. You can still see what God is doing there through Lisa's uncle Bishop Rick Thomas of Abundant life Christian centre. The church was started by her grandfather "Papa Woody" whom I spoke of earlier in this book. We saw many people saved in those days, which included the starting of the first Christian club in the history of Nova High school in Davie, Florida along with my best friend Robert Rotola, who is now a powerful pastor of Word of Life churches in Wichita, Kansas. If you are ever near there, don't miss the opportunity to be in a multi campus church that has a vision of twenty million souls by 2020.
During my early days, to be honest, I was so naive when it came to what went on behind closed doors in church. Truthfully, the backside of church is something I wish didn't exist and certainly never exposed. What I mean is,

though most of the people are pure, but there are elements of control, politics and power that undermine the innocence and purity of the people and ultimately the gospel. So for the most part my experience with church and people has been awesome. However, in order for you to understand my journey into the humble Upside of Down life I want to share some things that are going to be not only unveiling but also unnerving for me as well. I will do my best to share these hard things, doing my best to give honor in the midst of some very dishonorable actions and situations. These types of things I am sure has happened to many people in their journey and life and no one is perfect and without some scars. We must not blame or bash those who have hurt us but choose to release love and forgive- ness. Remember it is always the humble choice to be reconciled and much more important then being right. So let's get started. My wife and I began working in the ministry at a real young age. Lisa and I got married at eighteen and nineteen respectively and began to work in a new church plant with her father and mother. If you have ever been involved in planting a church you know that at the beginning you just need warm and faithful bodies to fill ministry positions that were not necessarily called, other than by the pastor who begs for their help. We were those recruited to work in the children's minis- try, where we quickly found our way while changing diapers, teaching and leading praise and worship to those who were mostly cute and a lot of fun. Not long after, the church began to grow, and I was now leading a youth group, which quickly grew to about one hundred kids, quite a phenomena for our size church. It was a totally mixed group of cultures ranging from White, Latin, and African Americans with also a touch of the islands, and a teen that came straight from England by the name of Josh Radford.

(Josh now is a powerful revivalist I highly recommend: www.revivallife.net)
Now my journey in this church was not a short time but over twenty-five years of working hard secularly, while serving as a full time pastor for the most part, without any pay. Today most people who serve in ministry expect some type of remuneration, but during those days, you served for free because you loved God. Now, I'm not saying it's wrong to pay people. We pay many very generously who serve faithfully with us in our work. It's just that in the day we cut our teeth in ministry, the compensation was never a determining or required factor for our service. When we moved into our new building, it was not without great trials. We had chosen to leave the com- fort of our almost ample, leased building, and for a time of almost three years the church went to a city center with only an outdoor space for our children so we could save the lease payment for the new facility. Besides that, the building that was supposed to take a year to build and 1.2 million ended up at 3 million dollars and a process of almost three years for too many numerous reasons to count.

From 1982 when my wife and I got married to 2002, my wife and I served the church faithfully and humbled ourselves lower and more often than I can really tell. I can remember working in my secular business, crying and dying inside as I begged God to please let me do the call I felt so strong of. To be quite honest, the prospect of me pastoring that church was actually getting dimmer each year. Though I was an associate pastor in name, I hardly ever got to preach and was now functioning as the worship leader. The only time I was really happy was when our senior pastor would go on a mission trip or vacation and I got to flow in my gifting. Finally, my dream would come true and my father-in-law told me that he was going to be moving out of state and was in the process of building a house. He hugged me, told me he loved me and that I was going to be the senior pastor of the church in just six months. The plan was that there would be a special service in January of 2002 where the reigns of the ministry would be handed over to Lisa and me. Now to be quite honest, I was concerned that I would not be received as the pastor because I hardly preached, and many people saw me as only the song leader. My father-in-law assured me that I would be preach- ing one time a month during the next six months, and then I was going to be the new senior pastor. Nothing much was discussed or planned, but I didn't care because the very thing God spoke to me on a bus in Germany was coming true! I didn't know this at the time, but my wife didn't believe her father was really going to move or give me the church, and she didn't have her hopes up. When the day of induction came, immediately following the service, her parents got in their car followed by a moving truck and left their church keys on the office counter. She was completely stunned, and we began to live our dream of pastoring and leading what we believed was a great work.

We started that first Sunday night with a special guest who would become our friends, Harry and Cheryl Salem. They ministered with passion, and they told us they sensed the fire in me burning. They were very encouraging. Lisa and I started out running with a vision that God gave me for the house of "Building the Kingdom, Healing the Hurting, and Touching the World." Something we were doing or being resonated with people, and we began to grow and grow. My style of leadership has always been of delegating to the best people and giving guidelines and boundaries but not specific details as to allow the person to accomplish the task with their personality, skill set and gifting. One of the things I tell people is that I don't want to micromanage you, and if I have to do that, you probably won't be with me long because I don't need another thing to do since I have a hard enough time just man- aging myself ! For those who don't know pastoring might be the hardest job in the world because of the great responsibility for countless lives and families who expect so much and yet sometimes give so little. I am not complaining just the nature of the call. It was during the four and a half years that we were the senior pastors that we saw the blessing of God poured out beyond our dreams.

As the church grew, we put on quality staff such as children's and worship pastors. We were also known in our community for outreach and helping our city. I can't tell you how much I loved my people, my church, and the privilege I had of pastoring them. The mandate God had given me of loving the people was being done, and the fruit was more than evident. Some of the highlights of the blessings were revival services with Tommie Zito, a revivalist who happened to be living in our city at the time and whom God used to radically change our lives with revival fire and radical evangelism. In three weeks our church saw, through street evangelism, over three thousand decision cards, miracles of salvation, rededication, and healing. My daughter, Brittney, and her now husband, AJ, were some of the teens who are today a product of that move of God that forever changed those touched by it. To be quite honest, the church was doing amazing. We were given another church building in the Miami area, and we renovated and partnered with another ministry to give it some of the finest pastors anywhere. We also bought a historic temple in the city center of the Nation of Panama for about $450,000, which was miraculously paid for with do debt from the generosity and heart of God's people in a short amount of time. It seemed like grace was generously abounding. I thought nothing could go wrong as the church had grown to almost 1,200 people on Sundays and the budget was over double than when my we began pastoring the church. During these years, we had the blessing of having some amazing musical guests like Israel and Mercy Me as well as some very well- known preachers like Jesse Duplantis and Tudor Bismark. To say the least, we were experiencing and living in a FOG (favor of God)!

I would love to say I have always lived in the power of humble and intentionally going lower but with all the success of the ministry I began to think nothing could ever go wrong. I was living my dream. I am not sure exactly how it happened but I must have allowed that stem of pride in somewhere, because what we had the privilege and blessing of growing and building was gone in less than 24 hours. To say it was humbling for us was an extreme understatement. This was an extreme low point in our lives but as we intentionally embraced going lower we believed God would one day take us higher and God did!

As we continued to lower ourselves a new dream was birthing and forming that was much bigger than just a large successful local church. (Not that there is anything wrong with that.) The dream and vision was to Save the Nations, the name of a new ministry and expanded vision and focus that was global and international as well as local. Though the journey hasn't always been easy, the kiss of heaven has used us to effect Nations. Some of those blessings include having helped fund and support a new church in St Petersburg Russia, where countless lives are being transformed by the power of the Gospel. Our greatest blessing to date is the formation of our first International Church in Rio Dejaneiro, Brazil. Through our spiritual son and daughter Miguel and Lilianny Ferreira who in just six services has seen a church grow to of over 200 people with there own building and official papers with the government. If you ever get a chance to go to Rio, you have to attend STN BRASIL. Please check them out at Facebook.com/savethenationsbrasil.

Since *the time of this writing a special couple Diego and Kelly have now become the pastors of the Brazil ministry and have expanded it to many House Churches and additional cities. Hallelujah!*

The Upside of Down life is intentionally going lower and that means you will eventually go higher. It's not just a principle it's a guarantee from the creator. And whoever exalts himself will be humbled, and he who humbles himself will be exalted. (Matthew 23:12 NKJV) This has been my Upside of Down journey, as you live your life always remember no matter what you go through and what you do remember to intentionally go lower before God. No matter what your past was like or those present challenges staring you down, God has promised that He would do you good in the end. As you live humble before God you can rest assured your highest and best will surely come. **It's the Upside of Down, How intentionally going lower will take your higher!**

Kenneth S. Albin

Notes

1.   http://www.merriam-webster.com/dictionary/humble
2.   http://www.blueletterbible.org/lang/lexicon/lexicon.cfm?Strongs=H6031&t=kjv
3,   http://www.thefreedictionary.com/apathy
4.   http://www.thefreedictionary.com/atrophy
5.   http://www.blueletterbible.org/lang/lexicon/lexicon.cfm?Strongs=H3966&t=kjv
6.   http://www.goodreads.com/quotes/326903-this-is-the-
legend-of-cassius-clay-the-most-beautiful
7.   http://www.blueletterbible.org/lang/lexicon/lexicon.cfm?Strongs=G5013&t=nkjv
8.   http://www.blueletterbible.org/lang/lexicon/lexicon.cfm?Strongs=G3813&t=kjv
9.   http://www.blueletterbible.org/lang/lexicon/lexicon.cfm?Strongs=G4762&t=kjv
10.   http://www.blueletterbible.org/lang/lexicon/lexicon.cfm?Strongs=H3384&t=KJV

11. http://www.blueletterbible.org/lang/lexicon/lexicon. cfm?Strongs=G2816&t=KJV

12. http://www.blueletterbible.org/lang/lexicon/lexicon. cfm?Strongs=G4239&t=KJV

13. http://www.merriam-webster.com/dictionary/inheritance

14. http://www.merriam-webster.com/dictionary/prideful

About the Author

Kenneth "Ken" Albin was born in New York, but moved to Florida as a young seven-year-old. Shortly after moving, Ken's parents were divorced, which left him deeply hurt for many years. During this time Ken, being Jewish, went to Hebrew school and Temple regularly. At the time of his thirteenth birthday and Bar Mitzvah, many confirmed a calling as a "rabbi" or "cantor" on his life.

It was soon after this that Ken's grandparents met the Lord at a Full Gospel businessmen's meeting. With momentum that came from above, Ken's father, David accepted the Lord, Jesus as his Savior. Being moved by his father's "born again" experience, Ken was now himself open to hear the message that so radically changed his dad's life. In the summer of Ken's sophomore year of high school, he gave his life to Jesus and his life was radically altered. He has been faithful to the house of God ever since. His mother, Racquel had also accepted Jesus and was now serving the Lord full time in Messianic ministry with her new husband, Rabbi Charles Kluge.

Ken has served in various areas of ministry including children's ministry, youth ministry and music ministry. He also has served in both associate and senior pastor roles for over twenty years. He has earned his Bachelor of Theology from International Seminary and his Master's Degree from Liberty University. He is also an accomplished singer/songwriter who has written over 100 songs. He loves to worship with the guitar and the keyboard.

Ken met his wife, Lisa at her grandfather's church in Margate, Florida. They were married when Lisa was just eighteen years of age. Six years later they welcomed their only child, Brittney into the world. Today Brittney and her husband, A.J. serve with Ken and Lisa in ministry and have a beautiful daughter, Brielle.

Ken and Lisa founded Save the Nations Church along with a handful of committed people who gathered in a home on September 17, 2006. God had put a vision in their hearts to reach the nations and bring light to a hurting world. Ken and Lisa currently serve as the overseeing pastors of the South Florida church campus in Broward County. As founders and pastors, they desire to inspire, instruct, resource and help people discover the destiny God has for them. The nations have become their home as together they travel to the nations, teaching, reviving and sharing the resources that help make influential disciples and bring people into appreciation of God's Torah, His "instructions."

Ken has always preached the word with the inspiration and revelation of the Holy Spirit. He has recently been on a journey to bring Christians into an understanding of the roots of their faith. "The Christian church has been hacked!" as Ken states in one of his latest books about restoring the inheritance and identity back to the church.

Presently, there are two international Save the Nations churches in Brazil: one in Rio and one in Marica'. Brazilian pastors, Diego and Kelly are doing an amazing work for God and great fruit is seen in that nation.

Ken has authored many books. All are available on Amazon. They are also being translated to Spanish, Portuguese and Russian languages.

BOOKS BY KENNETH S. ALBIN

YOU ARE BORN FOR THE EXTRAORDINARY

UPSIDE OF DOWN

THE MYSTERY OF THE CROWN

HACKED: THE HEBREW CHRISTIAN

THE PASSOVER BLESSING

HANNUKAH AND PURIM ARE FOR CHRISTIANS TOO!

HIT THE MARK

HIDDEN BLESSINGS REVEALED

TABERNACLES ITS A CELEBRATION AND NOT JUST AN OPTION

CHRISTIANS GET TO CELEBRATE PASSOVER TOO!

Contact Information: for Ken & Lisa Albin
 www.savethenations.com / www.hitthemarktorah.tv
info@savethenations.com

Christians

GET TO CELEBRATE

Passover

TOO!

Learning its Secrets, Power
and Abundant Blessings

KENNETH S. ALBIN

THE MYSTERY

OF THE CROWN

"WHY CHRIST HAD TO RECEIVE IT &
HOW ITS SECRETS CAN CHANGE YOUR WORLD."

FOREWORD BY TED SHUTTLESWORTH

KENNETH STEVEN ALBIN

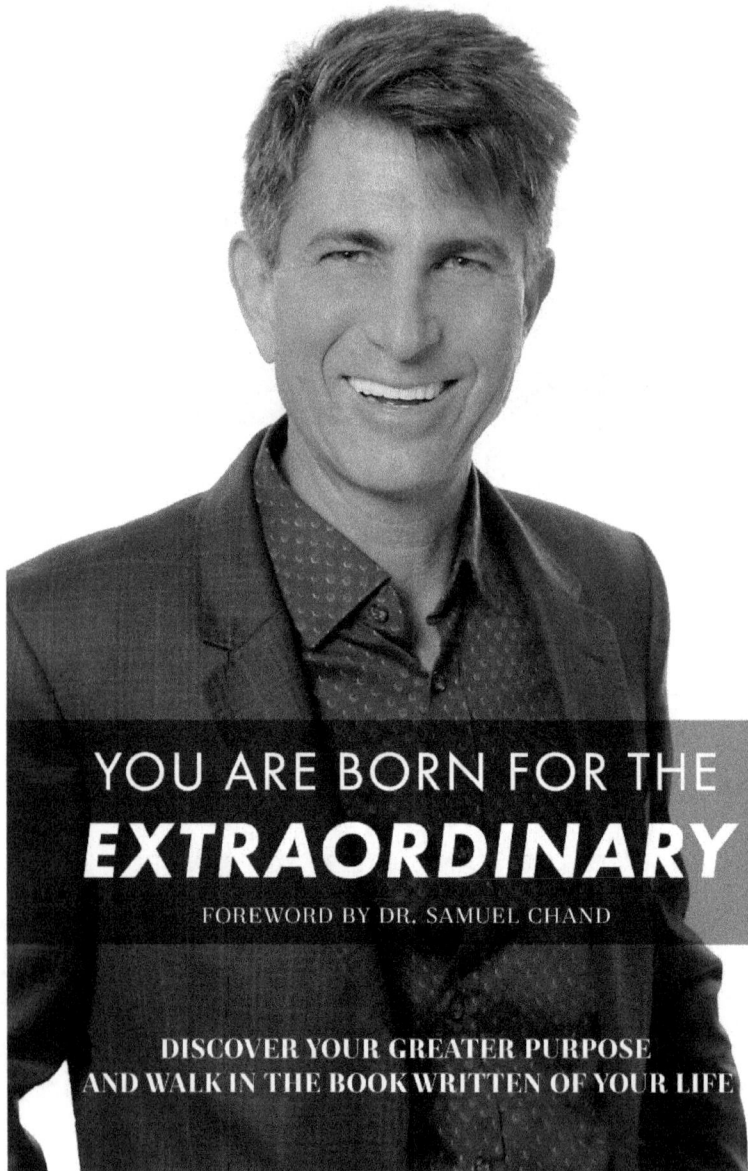

YOU ARE BORN FOR THE
EXTRAORDINARY

FOREWORD BY DR. SAMUEL CHAND

DISCOVER YOUR GREATER PURPOSE
AND WALK IN THE BOOK WRITTEN OF YOUR LIFE

HACKED

ז
פריצה
ה
י
ת

RESTORING
STOLEN IDENTITY
AND EMBRACING THE
INHERITED BLESSING

THE HEBREW CHRISTIAN

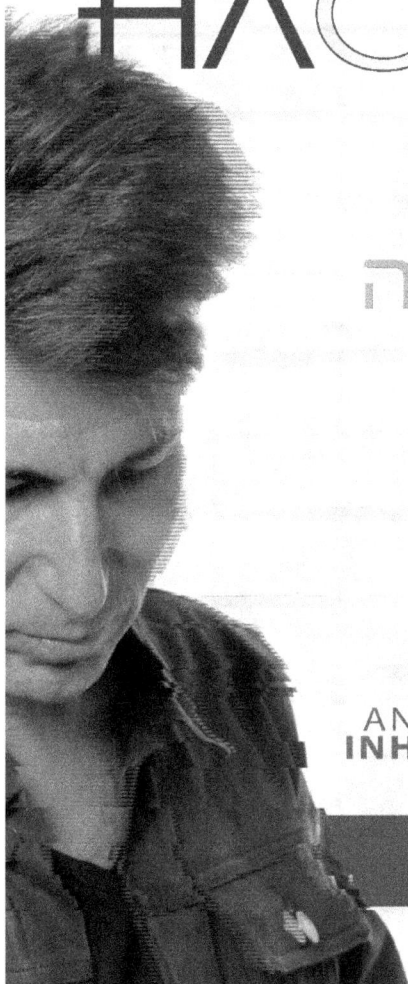

HIT THE MARK

How Christians can walk in the mysteries of the Torah

And receive all its blessings

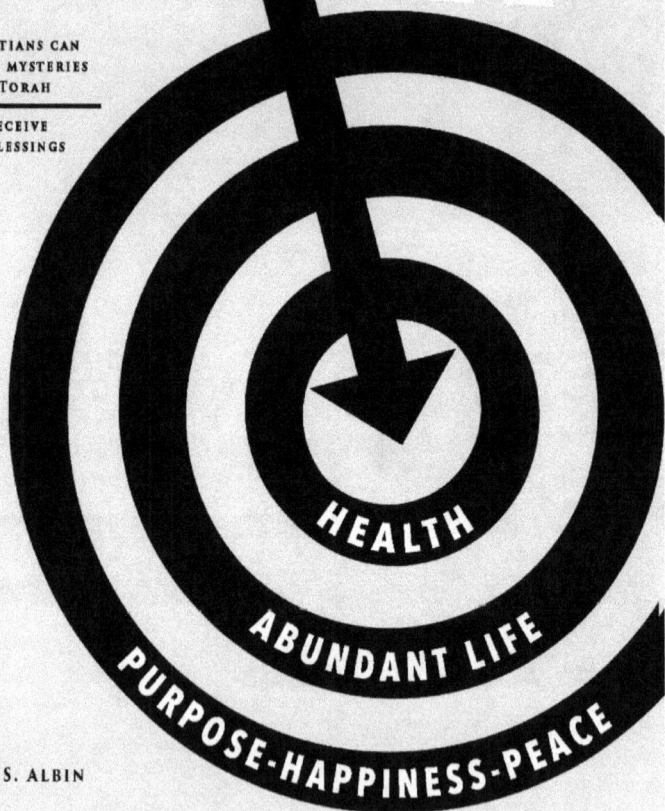

HEALTH

ABUNDANT LIFE

PURPOSE-HAPPINESS-PEACE

Kenneth S. Albin

No More Leaven!

The Blessings Christians Receive By Celebrating The Feast Of Unleavened Bread

By Kenneth S. Albin

TABERNACLES

IT'S A CELEBRATION & *NOT* JUST AN OPTION!

How Christians can
celebrate this Biblical Feast
and the True Birthday of Messiah

BY KENNETH S. ALBIN

HID DEN BLESS INGS

REVEALED

A Christian Understanding for Celebrating
the Biblical Holidays of Rosh Hashanah and Yom Kippur

BY KENNETH S. ALBIN

HANUKKAH
and PURIM
ARE FOR CHRISTIANS TOO!

KENNETH S. ALBIN

www.ingramcontent.com/pod-product-compliance
Lightning Source LLC
LaVergne TN
LVHW051228080426
835513LV00016B/1470